Cambridge Elements

Elements in Religion and Monotheism
edited by
Paul K. Moser
Loyola University Chicago
Chad Meister
*Affiliate Scholar, Ansari Institute for Global Engagement with Religion,
University of Notre Dame*

MONOTHEISM AND MIRACLE

Eric Eve
Harris Manchester College, Oxford

Shaftesbury Road, Cambridge CB2 8EA, United Kingdom

One Liberty Plaza, 20th Floor, New York, NY 10006, USA

477 Williamstown Road, Port Melbourne, VIC 3207, Australia

314–321, 3rd Floor, Plot 3, Splendor Forum, Jasola District Centre, New Delhi – 110025, India

103 Penang Road, #05–06/07, Visioncrest Commercial, Singapore 238467

Cambridge University Press is part of Cambridge University Press & Assessment, a department of the University of Cambridge.

We share the University's mission to contribute to society through the pursuit of education, learning and research at the highest international levels of excellence.

www.cambridge.org
Information on this title: www.cambridge.org/9781009547871

DOI: 10.1017/9781009386500

© Eric Eve 2025

This publication is in copyright. Subject to statutory exception and to the provisions of relevant collective licensing agreements, no reproduction of any part may take place without the written permission of Cambridge University Press & Assessment.

When citing this work, please include a reference to the DOI 10.1017/9781009386500

First published 2025

A catalogue record for this publication is available from the British Library

ISBN 978-1-009-54787-1 Hardback
ISBN 978-1-009-38654-8 Paperback
ISSN 2631-3014 (online)
ISSN 2631-3006 (print)

Cambridge University Press & Assessment has no responsibility for the persistence or accuracy of URLs for external or third-party internet websites referred to in this publication and does not guarantee that any content on such websites is, or will remain, accurate or appropriate.

Monotheism and Miracle

Elements in Religion and Monotheism

DOI: 10.1017/9781009386500
First published online: February 2025

Eric Eve
Harris Manchester College, Oxford
Author for correspondence: Eric Eve, eric.eve@hmc.ox.ac.uk

Abstract: *Monotheism implies a God* who is active in creation. An author writing a novel provides a better analogy for God's creative activity than an artificer constructing a mechanism. A miracle is then not an interruption of the ordinary course of nature so much as a divine decision to do something out of the ordinary, and miracle is primarily a narrative category. We perceive as miracles events that are extraordinary while also fitting our understanding of divine purpose. Many miracle accounts may remain problematic, however, since recognizing that a given story purports to narrate a miracle does not determine whether the miracle occurred. This Element suggests weighing competing narratives. In doing so the understanding of the normal workings of nature will carry considerable weight. Nevertheless, there can be instances where believers may, from their own faith perspective, be justified in concluding that a miracle has occurred.

Keywords: miracle, monotheism, narrative, religion, belief

© Eric Eve 2025

ISBNs: 9781009547871 (HB), 9781009386548 (PB), 9781009386500 (OC)
ISSNs: 2631-3014 (online), 2631-3006 (print)

Contents

1 Preliminaries   1

2 Narrative Approaches   9

3 Examples of Miracles   29

4 Assessing Miracles   43

5 Conclusion   58

   Bibliography   60

1 Preliminaries

1.1 Introduction

Stories of miracles are found in many religions, not least in the three major monotheistic (Abrahamic) faiths: Judaism, Christianity, and Islam.[1] Such stories may evoke belief, scepticism, curiosity, or puzzlement. To one person, the story of a prophet, saint, or founder figure performing such seemingly impossible feats as walking on water or curing the sick through no known medical means may signify little more than the credulity of religious people and the patent falsehood of religious claims, while to another it may reinforce their faith by testifying to the truth of their beliefs, while to yet another it may be little more than a curiosity that has little impact on their belief or unbelief.

It would be tempting, but facile, to suggest that people in the past were more credulous and liable to believe all sorts of nonsense while we moderns are more knowledgeable, sophisticated, and critical, but this would be an oversimplification at best. Scepticism, doubt, curiosity, and belief have existed alongside one another from antiquity to the present day. The proportions may have changed over time, in part due to rising levels of education, the secularization of the modern West, and the intellectual inheritance of the Enlightenment, but the extent of the change may not be so great as is popularly imagined. The views of published intellectuals and academics may not always reflect those of the wider public, and the views of Western intellectuals are unlikely to reflect those of the world at large.

Even people who consider themselves as enlightened modern Western sceptics may find themselves praying for a miracle in the face of trying circumstances, such as serious illness. Conversely, some devout believers may be naturally sceptical towards the miraculous. One does not need to believe that Jesus walked on water to be guided by his command to love one's neighbour as oneself, and the urgent task of feeding today's hungry is not obviously advanced by insisting that Jesus and Moses were both able to do so by miraculous means. Many people of faith may consider that focusing on miracles is a distraction from more practical ways of furthering God's work in the world. Others will disagree.

The aim of this *Element* is not to survey the attitude to the miraculous in the various monotheistic faiths, but to explore some of the key issues that arise in connection with miracles within a monotheistic framework. Given both a monotheistic framework of belief and a commitment to the modern scientific view of the universe, can one give an account of divine action in the world that

---

[1] For a survey of miracles in all the major world religions, see Woodward, *The Book of Miracles* and Part III of Twelftree (ed.), *The Cambridge Companion to Miracles*.

allows for miracle? How are accounts of miracles to be evaluated? What sort of significance might they have? It might be thought that an omnipotent (all-powerful) God can do anything God chooses, so that monotheism automatically implies the possibility of miracle, but is that the case? And even if we know that God *could* in principle work miracles, can we be sure that God chooses to do so?

Before we can even begin to address such questions, we must first clarify what we mean by the two key terms involved: monotheism and miracle.

1.2 Monotheism

Monotheism can be defined simply as the belief in one God, but the term normally implies something about the nature of this God, namely that God is eternal, all-powerful, all-knowing, all-loving, that God is the Creator of all that is, and that God transcends creation, meaning that God exists both independently of and beyond creation; the physical universe depends on God for its existence but God in no way depends on the physical universe for God's existence.

We should distinguish mono*theism* from mono*deism*. Deism is the belief that God acted only to create the universe at its inception, and that the universe then continues to run as an autonomous system according to its own laws without any further divine intervention. Such a creator God is wholly transcendent. Theism, on the other hand, holds that God acts not just at the point of creation but remains active in creation, maintaining and guiding it at every point. The God of theism, therefore, can be said to be both transcendent and immanent, both outside and independent of creation but also active and in some sense present within it.

Deism would seem to exclude the possibility of miracle, since in a deistic system, once God has created the universe, the universe is left to carry on as an autonomous system according to its inherent laws, and there is little scope for its wholly transcendent God to intervene directly to perform a miracle. One could imagine such a God so designing the universe that it would throw up what some people take to be miracles of its own accord, but the perception of such events as miracles would rely on their beholders' ignorance of the deeper complexities at work in the natural order, or else would require a rigid determinism in which everything had been tightly preordained in the initial design of the system to produce apparent miracles just when they were needed. Such ideas could be explored further, but here we are concerned with miracles in a theistic context.

Mono*theism* would seem more hospitable to miracles, since an all-powerful God who is continually active within creation could presumably make the physical universe behave in whatever way God wills, which could include miraculous events. Yet it has been observed that theism needs to be at least tinged with deism in order to avoid collapsing into pantheism. Theism maintains a distinction between God and creation such that the created order is something other than God's physical manifestation and that God's maintenance of creation affords it at least some measure of autonomy. This surely places some limits on the ways in which God could be continually active within creation, limits we could explore by asking what a theistic God can either do or will if God is to be consistent with God's own nature.

Such limits have often been illustrated through examples of logically impossible actions, such as God drawing a square circle, creating a weight that is too heavy for God to lift, or making twelve a prime number. Rather than getting drawn into the debate over whether omnipotence includes the ability to do the logically impossible, it will suffice to question whether 'making twelve a prime number' is any more a coherent description of an action than 'eating a prime number' so the issue may be more about what verbal formulations make sense than about limitations on divine action.

More germane to the matter of monotheism and miracle are descriptions of actions that an omnipotent God could in principle perform but which nevertheless may strike most people as problematic, for example:

- God can break God's promises.
- God can act foolishly and irresponsibly.
- God can do evil for the sheer sadistic pleasure of it.
- God can act to thwart God's own purposes.
- God can behave contrary to God's nature.

The last element in this list summarizes what is likely to be felt problematic about the preceding four. It is logically possible that an all-powerful Creator could be capricious and inconsistent, but would such a Being conform to what most monotheists understand by the term 'God'? A God who is not only all-powerful but all-wise, all-just and all-loving must surely be a God who can be relied upon to act in ways that are consistent with this characterization. We may not know exactly how God's love, justice, and wisdom should work out in practice, but if such descriptions of God are to have any meaning at all, they must surely imply something recognizable as what humans would call love, justice, and wisdom.

The question is then not whether an all-powerful God *can* work miracles, but whether God might choose to or be able to do so without thwarting God's own purposes or contradicting God's own nature. Since a theistic God is believed to be constantly active in maintaining and upholding creation, it might appear self-defeating for God to perform miracles that go against the very laws of nature God is busily upholding. Moreover, in order for a loving God to afford a measure of autonomy to morally accountable sentient creatures, God must provide them with a stable and reliable environment in which rational actors can behave with reasonably predictable consequences. For humans to flourish requires a stable and dependable environment, so that any God who takes responsibility for maintaining creation needs to play by the rules God has laid down.

Raising this question does not settle it, however, not least since the obvious counterargument would be that God could surely perform the odd miracle here or there without any risk of the cosmos collapsing into chaos or undermining the ability of free moral agents to act. To take an obvious example, it is hard to see how either the coherence of creation or human ability to plan and act would be undermined if someone you love is miraculously cured of terminal cancer, or if a humanitarian charity doing superb work receives a totally unexpected and transformational donation in response to prayer. Yet this counterargument is itself vulnerable to counterarguments. If miraculous cures to terminal cancer become common, might there not be a risk of removing incentives to research effective medical cures, so undermining human responsibility and initiative (and the possibility of curing sufferers who don't happen to have people praying for them)? But if miraculous cures remain sufficiently rare that cancer research continues unabated, on what basis can a just and loving God decide to cure Patient A but not Patients B, C, D . . . and Z? While such arguments do not settle the matter, they do raise questions that need to be probed further.

A different issue is how we envisage the nature of divine causation involved in working a miracle. The potential danger here is thinking along the lines of 'This event is inexplicable in human terms; no human can have brought it about, and no natural process can have brought it about, therefore only God can have done it'. The problem here is not that this is necessarily wrong, but that it risks placing God's action in the same category as human action and natural causation. Can that be right? Surely what monotheism understands by God is not just one actor alongside other actors or one cause alongside other causes, but an agent of a quite different kind. The problem with a 'God of the gaps' is not just that such a God risks diminishment as advances in human knowledge shrink the gaps, but that the gaps are conceived as lacunae within the natural order, not as something fundamentally transcendent, and that if God acts not only to set creation in motion but also to uphold and maintain it, then God's action is to be found throughout creation, and not just in the parts humans currently struggle to explain. Whatever divine action consists of, it must be something of a wholly different order from human action or natural causation. We shall be suggesting that a narrative or authorial analogy may be a more helpful way of conceiving such divine action than a divine clockmaker model that effectively envisages God intervening by tinkering with the mechanism as if he were another physical entity standing alongside the clock. But first, we should examine what we mean by 'miracle'.

1.3 Miracle

The discussion has so far treated the term 'miracle' as if it straightforwardly meant an exception to the normal course of events – a breach of the laws of nature. But although miracle is commonly conceived in these terms, and much discussion of miracle (classically going back to Hume and beyond)[2] has proceeded as if this is what the term 'miracle' principally meant, there are several reasons why this may be unhelpful.

The first is that it does not reflect the way the word 'miracle' is often used. On the one hand, it leaves out the requirement that to count as a miracle, some meaningful action by God is required, and on the other, people often count as miracles events that do not obviously contravene any known laws of nature. The charity that receives an unexpectedly large donation in response to prayer might well regard it as a miracle, but no one involved thinks any fundamental law of physics has been contravened. The person who recovers unexpectedly from terminal cancer may surprise their physicians, who may in turn struggle to come up with a medical explanation, but maybe the sheer complexity of the workings of the human body and the way the human mind interacts with it would make it impossible for medical science to point to any law of nature that had been clearly broken. Likewise, the person whose life is transformed by a chance meeting with a stranger might well look back on that meeting as a miracle, although here a breach of the laws of nature isn't remotely in view. While someone might object that such events are not 'real miracles', these are all ways in which the term 'miracle' might be used by people who believe that a miracle has occurred. The common thread in all these cases is that something wonderfully unexpected has taken place, which the person or persons concerned are unwilling to ascribe to pure chance and which to them appear to be the result of divine action on their behalf, or for the furtherance of God's design. While supposed breaches of the laws of nature often feature in discussions of miracle, this is not always the case, and there is in fact no generally agreed definition of miracle (just as there is no generally agreed sharp dividing line between miracle and providence).[3]

The second reason is that a definition involving breaches of the laws of nature does not correspond to anything in the Jewish, Christian, or Moslem scriptures, which supply many of the classic miracle stories in their respective monotheistic

---

[2] See Section X, 'On Miracle' in Hume, *Enquiries*.
[3] For the difficulties in finding an agreed definition of miracle, see Basinger, 'What Is a Miracle', pp. 19–35. For objections to defining miracle as a breach of the laws of nature, see Larmer, 'The Meanings of Miracle', pp. 36–53, with which compare Hesse, 'Miracles and the Laws of Nature', pp. 35–42; and Keener, *Miracles*, Vol. I, pp. 128–38. Levine, 'Miracles and the Laws of Nature', pp. 128–51, argues that it is unhelpful to discuss miracle in relation to the laws of nature and that the more relevant issues are the nature of causation and divine action.

traditions. Indeed, no biblical writer uses a word corresponding to the modern English 'miracle' in any such sense. This in part is because no biblical writer operated with a modern (post-Enlightenment) conception of nature as an autonomous closed system running according to its own fixed laws. The biblical authors saw God as much at work in the regular workings of creation as in surprising exceptions to it. They also tended to see God as exercising power, not through tinkering with an otherwise deterministic mechanism but by exercising his sovereign power of command. At the beginning of Genesis, God acts by commanding creation into existence: 'Let there be light.' Jesus often also performs miracles through commands: 'Who then is this that even wind and sea obey him?' (Mark 4:39-41). God is the lord of creation, which is God's for God to command. The notion that God may be contravening some fundamental law of physics is simply not in the sacred texts.

The third reason is the problematic nature of the term 'laws of nature' and hence 'breach of the laws of nature'. Does the term 'laws of nature' refer to how nature actually behaves (which may be different from our current scientific understanding) or how nature is currently understood to behave (in which case 'laws of nature' means something like 'the current best generally agreed set of scientific theories', which may not be entirely correct or complete)? If 'laws of nature' means the former, then a breach of the laws of nature would imply nature not behaving as nature actually behaves, which is simply nonsensical. If it means the latter, then it leaves open the possibility that our current scientific theories are not entirely correct, so that a breach may occur whenever something happens that our current theories can't account for, including occurrences that indicate that our theories may need correcting.

Richard Swinburne offers a potentially helpful way round the latter difficulty by suggesting a distinction between repeatable and non-repeatable exceptions to current scientific understanding, with miracle applying only to the latter.[4] For example, the orbit of Mercury conforms better with Einstein's Theory of General Relativity than with Newton's theory of gravity, and so before Einstein's theory became established, the orbit of Mercury would have constituted a breach of the laws of nature as described by Isaac Newton. It is a *repeatable* breach, however, because observations of the orbit of Mercury can be repeated as often as one might wish and always yield the same result, as might other observations that conform to General Relativity better than Newtonian mechanics, such as the bending of starlight round the sun. It is this consistent repeatability that make such exceptions to what was previously believed to be a law of nature evidence for a need to move to a better theory rather than evidence for miracle. On the other

---

[4] Swinburne, *Concept of Miracle*, pp. 26–29.

hand, raising people from the dead, turning water into wine, or feeding 5,000 people with 5 loaves and 2 fishes would appear to be unique or at least extremely rare events that cannot be regularly repeated and hence explained by a better physical theory, and so are properly understood as miracles.

This only takes us so far, however, since there are at least two considerations that might prevent an otherwise unrepeatable exception to the laws of nature counting as a miracle. The first is if it should appear to be a random freak occurrence: for example, if Mercury briefly wobbled in its orbit for no apparent reason whatsoever and the phenomenon was not witnessed again and this weirdly irregular behaviour conveyed absolutely nothing of any religious significance to anyone. This would be an inexplicable event, but it would not obviously be a miracle.

The second is that the laws of nature, or physical theories, can only tell us what will happen if nothing unexpected intervenes. Perhaps Mercury's temporary wobble might be caused by an encounter with a form of matter or energy we do not yet understand, or by a race of super-powerful aliens deploying tractor beams from invisible star ships because it amuses them to play pranks on lesser species who think they know it all.

This leads to another problem. When someone speaks of the laws of nature, are they thinking of fundamental laws of physics such as Schrödinger's Wave Equation or the Second Law of Thermodynamics, or are they merely referring to the normal course of events that such laws are believed to underpin? Discussion of miracles often cite walking on water or bringing the dead back to life as clear examples of breaches of the laws of nature, but these examples are not couched in the same terms as those in which fundamental laws of physics are formulated. In the first case, it is surely conceivable that someone could come up with a device (a jet pack or buoyancy boots, say) that would allow people to walk on water without contravening any fundamental laws of physics. Even in the second it could be argued that since the fundamental physical processes underlying death and decay at the atomic level are in principle reversible, it is conceivable that technological advances might one day allow such processes to be reversed. It would no doubt be far harder than turning omelettes back into eggs (which, so far as I know, has never been achieved), but provided the reduction in entropy in the resuscitated corpse was matched by a corresponding increase in entropy elsewhere (say in the nanobots that were deployed to effect the revival of the corpse) no fundamental laws of physics need have been breached. This is not to suggest that (at least at any time up to the present) raising the dead might be any less miraculous, but to suggest the possibility that its miraculous nature could be due to something other than a breach of the laws of nature. We might clarify this through a different example.

It would have been physically impossible for St Paul to appear before his congregation in Corinth to address them while he was imprisoned in Rome, but the reason for this is not because it would have breached the laws of nature but because Paul lacked access to videoconferencing technology.

To be sure, there may be some purported miracles that would violate some fundamental physical laws had they occurred, but in most cases the issue is not so much any breach of the fundamental laws of nature (as we currently understand them) as the occurrence of an event that could almost certainly not occur spontaneously and which is beyond current human ability to bring about (or would have been at the time it was said to have taken place). This is not to make such events any more plausible, but to suggest that their implausibility usually rests not in clear exceptions to the fundamental laws of physics but in the absence of any causes sufficient to make them occur.

While there is no generally agreed definition of miracle, it will be helpful to propose one to use here. For the purposes of our present discussion, we shall define miracle as 'an otherwise seemingly inexplicable event attributed to divine action that is taken to be religiously meaningful and appropriate'.[5] This clearly introduces elements of subjectivity into the definition, but this is inevitable, since the perception of miracle can only be relative to people's knowledge and beliefs. It does not, however, necessarily rest on individual subjectivity, since it more commonly involves the intersubjectivity of groups who share the relevant knowledge and beliefs.[6]

The three elements of this definition must be taken in concert. An event is seemingly inexplicable if it appears beyond what nature or known agents can plausibly bring about, or if it involves too much of a coincidence. To count as a miracle, it must also be attributed to divine action. For the attribution to divine action to appear as the most plausible explanation the putative event must be in accord with what is known or believed about the nature of the God to whom it is attributed and to have some kind of appropriate religious significance. Thus, for example, to gain a wholly unexpected financial windfall in response to prayer to spend on charitable purposes might count as a miracle, whereas to gain the same windfall in response to prayer to purchase a luxury yacht for one's own selfish enjoyment would not, just as the sudden inexplicable cure of a loved one would be a far more plausible candidate for a miracle than the seemingly inexplicable demise of one's objectionable neighbour.

I suggest, therefore, that it's best to distinguish the concept of *anomaly* (a seemingly inexplicable event in defiance of what is known of the laws of nature) from that of *miracle* (as just defined). While some miracles would

---

[5] Cf. Woodward, *Book of Miracles*, p. 29.   [6] Cf. the discussion in Tennant, *Miracle*, pp. 73–75.

also be anomalies if they occurred, an anomaly is not necessarily a miracle, and a miracle is not necessarily an anomaly. These two terms belong to different areas of discourse, the one scientific and the other religious. *Miracle* is not a concept primarily to do with natural science; it is a relational concept concerned with how a believer or group of believers perceive their relationship to God and God's actions on their or God's behalf. In what follows we shall be arguing that this conception is best captured in a *narrative* concept of miracle. The relationship between miracle and anomaly (where the two potentially overlap) is an issue to which we shall return in the final section. Meanwhile, readers interested in further exploring the philosophical and scientific issues at stake in envisioning how divine action could intervene in the natural order may wish to consult Jeffrey Koperski's lucid treatment.[7]

Note finally that the definition of miracle offered here means that in discussing the possibility of miracle, we shall primarily be occupied with the epistemological question of whether, and if so when, we might be justified in believing that miracles have occurred. Since this Element is concerned with examining miracle from the perspective of monotheistic belief, the metaphysical question of the possibility of miracle is largely settled by definition: monotheism implies belief in an omnipotent God, which in turn implies a God able to work miracles if God so chooses. The question whether God might so choose cannot be answered absent beliefs about how God in fact acts, which in turn depend on the contents of specific faith traditions and how we go about evaluating the claims they make.

2 Narrative Approaches

2.1 Narrative as Explanatory Category

Many people today regard natural science as the paradigmatic explanatory framework; in other words, scientific explanations, framed in terms of the laws of nature (or in terms of the best current scientific theories), are taken to be the most cogent ones, the 'proper' explanations of how and why things happen the way they do. Moreover, among scientific theories, it is often fundamental theories of physics, expressed in mathematical equations such as $E = mc^2$, that are taken as the paradigmatic form of theory, since they offer neat, concise, and often elegant formulations and the promise of precision, the ability to calculate results that can be tested and used for wide range of practical purposes.

---

[7] Koperski, *Divine Action, Determinism, and the Laws of Nature*; this can be downloaded as a free PDF.

Not all scientific theories are of this form, however, and not everything of interest to human existence can be captured in equations or reduced to what is precisely measurable. Sciences like biology and medicine (let alone social sciences such as economics, sociology, and anthropology) cannot live by equations alone but must often rely on descriptions and narratives. To understand human societies, human bodies, and even human-made machines is often to understand something about their structures, how the parts relate to one another and the whole and how they contribute to the functioning of the whole. Some theories even in relatively hard sciences effectively involve narratives (stories). Darwin's theory of evolution by natural selection offers a narrative of how species developed over time. As such it offered an alternative story to that found in the early chapters of Genesis or by other accounts of evolution. Cosmological theories about the origins of the universe likewise offer a narrative that begins with a Big Bang, followed by a period of rapid expansion (or 'inflation') and then the coalescing of matter into stars and galaxies, the formation of heavier elements in the stars, and so on. If such theories prove satisfying to the layman (and perhaps also to many scientists), it is because they offer stories that seem to make sense.

Narrative is one of the oldest and most prevalent ways in which we human beings organize information to make sense of ourselves and the world in which we live. It is surely no accident that it is narratives such as the poetic epics ascribed to Homer that stand at the fount of Western literature, (similar examples could no doubt be found in other cultures). It is stories that provide our sense of individual and collective identity, and stories that guide our hopes for the future and hence actions in the present.[8] The stories we absorb from what we read, watch, and listen to (whether factual or fictional, whether from literature, film, TV, news, historical drama, or speculative fiction) shape our ideas of what is or is not acceptable, which models we might want to follow, and what constitutes the good life, whether that be one of instant gratification and the path to fame and riches or one of hard work, or dedication to artistic or intellectual endeavour, or long-term romantic relationships, or service to others. It is stories that shape our sense of what is heroic or cowardly, commendable or despicable. It is through stories that we can gain empathy and understanding of what makes our fellow human beings tick, or else be encouraged to treat them as objects for our own greed, gratification, and advancement.

A narrative is not simply a list of events in chronological order. A narrative gives a sequential account of events which, implicitly or explicitly, attempts to

---

[8] On the centrality of narrative for understanding personal and Christian communal identity, see Stroup, *The Promise of Narrative Theology*, pp. 100–13 & pp. 132–98 respectively; see p. 245 for narrative as the principal way of apprehending God.

trace connections between them to show how or why things happened the way they did, and also, perhaps, whether things could have worked out differently, and how both the outcome and the way it was reached should be evaluated. A well-constructed narrative often doesn't need to spell out explicitly that A caused B and C prevented D; stories can often rely on well-established narrative conventions and background knowledge for their audiences to fill in the causal gaps by themselves. If, in the opening scene of a novel, a corpse is discovered with a bullet hole in the middle of its forehead, the narrator does not need to spell out that a murder has just been committed and that the plot is probably going to involve identifying the killer, nor does the narrative need to go to great lengths to explain that a murderer is likely to have a motive such as greed, jealousy, hatred, or revenge.

A story does not need to be literally true to help us orient ourselves in the world. Conversely, calling something a story in no way determines whether it is true or false. What is meant by calling a story true or false is in any case a complex question we cannot do justice to here. Correspondence to the facts can only be part of the answer. Truth may not always be the same as fact, so that, for example, even a purely fictitious story may point to an important truth if it shows us something about the human condition or inspires us to act in more noble and humane ways. Conversely, a broadly factual account may badly mislead if contrives to distort causal connections or impute dubious motives or omit crucial information.

Many religions, including monotheistic ones, primarily understand themselves and God through stories. The God of the Hebrew Scriptures (aka 'Old Testament') is primarily known through God's acts, the stories about God's dealings with humankind and in particular with Israel. There are passages in which God is described according to God's attributes (e.g., Exod. 34:6-7), but these would have little impact apart from the narratives in which they are embedded, and especially such foundational acts of God such as the exodus in which Israel is delivered from slavery, tested and forged in the wilderness, given the covenant at Mount Sinai, and led to the Promised Land. Likewise, the foundational texts of Christianity include four narrative accounts of the ministry of Jesus and one of the birth and spread of the early church (the four gospels and Acts), along with an apocalypse that includes a series of visions in the form of short narratives. Even the more discursive epistles often contain elements of implicit or explicit narrative. Paul's letter to the Romans, for example, both expounds and presupposes a narrative in which the God of Israel sent God's son to die on the Cross to reconcile humankind to Godself. It also includes a section (Romans 9–11) reviewing the narrative of God's dealings with Israel designed to show that God is staying true to God's promises by offering salvation through Jesus Christ culminating in a brief narrative of the ultimate salvation of Jew and Gentile alike. The epistle concludes with a short narrative account of Paul's missionary activities and future plans (Romans 15:18-32). The Jesus of the Synoptic Gospels (Matthew, Mark, and Luke) often chose to teach through the medium of short stories, namely the parables.

So, while doctrines, dogma, theological debate, and philosophical speculation all have their place in religious belief, the most fundamental, foundational category is story. Without narrative, we'd have no clear idea of who Abraham, Moses, Jesus, or Mohammed were, or, indeed, of who the God of Abraham, Isaac, and Jacob is; we'd be left only with thin abstractions of little religious power. Given that narrative is a fundamental explanatory category both of human cognition in general and religious understanding in particular, not least in monotheistic belief, it will be worth exploring narrative models of creation, divine action, and miracle.

2.2 Creation as Narrative

2.2.1 Storytelling as a Model of Creation

To understand what we mean by describing God as Creator, we have (explicitly or implicitly) to resort to some human analogy. To describe God as making heaven and earth could easily conjure up the image of a human artificer, a carpenter, builder, architect, or engineer, perhaps. Following the Enlightenment and the explanations of nature offered by Newtonian mechanics, it seemed natural to liken the act of creation to that of clockmaker constructing an intricate mechanism. Even if such a model is officially disavowed, it can often form the implicit model of creation we work with. The physical universe then appears to be an autonomous system, like a machine, organism, or building. God designed and built this machine (or organism or building), which means the act of creation lies way back in the past. God now stands outside this universe that God made way back when, so that any direct divine action in the present would involve God tinkering with creation (inviting the question why God didn't get it right in the first place) or else 'interfering' with it in some way analogous to a clockmaker poking around inside his clock with a screwdriver. While many people may reject such crude images, in the absence of anything better, they risk being what we fall back on by default.

I'd like to suggest that a better (although necessarily imperfect) analogy for divine creation and divine action is storytelling, the creation of a *narrative*. Although in principle this narrative could take the form of a film or play, or even a different kind of artistic expression altogether, such as a musical composition, for the purposes of the present discussion we shall mainly envisage creation on the analogy of an author writing a novel.[9]

---

[9] I owe this idea to Sayers, *Mind*.

On this analogy God is the Author who writes the (many layered and highly complex) story that is the universe, and human beings (and other creatures) are characters in the story. The composition of a narrative isn't simply about the characters and the things they do and say (even if this usually forms the foreground). Telling a story, especially one that takes place in an unfamiliar setting, also involves world-building, the construction of a coherent environment in which the action takes place. A well-known example would be *The Lord of the Rings* trilogy, which not only tells the story of Frodo and Gandalf and their companions in the War of the Ring but also takes place in the fictious land of Middle-Earth, whose geography, history, ethnography, myths, legends, and even languages Tolkien worked out in painstaking detail. Narratives involve settings as much as characters and events, and the settings must be coherent if the narrative is to make sense.

It may be objected that the universe is nothing like a novel and that we human beings are not characters in a story but real people. These objections do have some force, and we shall address some of the limitations of the analogy shortly. An analogy is, after all, just an analogy, and analogies should never be pressed too far. That said, from the perspective of the characters within a well-constructed narrative, both they and the other characters within the story are fully real, just as the world they live in is fully real (even if they may from time to time reflect that 'All the world's a stage').[10] But before addressing the potential limitations of this authorial model, we should first consider its advantages.

2.2.2 Advantages of the Narrative Model

Taking creation to be more akin to writing a novel than to building a machine has several advantages for a monotheistic understanding of God. These include:

1. Like the God of monotheism, an author is fully transcendent in relation to his or her story. The story depends on the author for its existence; the author does not depend on the story for his or hers. Likewise, the author is outside the time and space of the story.
2. Like the God of monotheism, an author can nevertheless also be immanent in his or her story. A story may reveal something about the author, such as the author's worldview and values. An author can even become incarnate in his or her story, if the author wishes, by writing himself or herself into the narrative as one of its characters.
3. Authors create their entire stories from beginning to end; they do not merely write the opening line and expect the story to unfold of its own accord. They are more like the God of monotheism, active at every point in their creation

---

[10] Shakespeare, *As You Like It*, Act II Scene VII Line 139.

throughout its timespan than the God of deism who just creates a mechanism and sets it going.

4. Like the God of monotheism, an author is fully omnipotent and omniscient with respect to his or her creation. Within their narrative authors can, in principle, make anything happen they wish to happen and know everything they wish to know about the actions, settings, characters, and other elements of their story.

5. While some human authors may write for financial gain or fame, it is perfectly possible to tell a story just for the love of doing so. Storytelling thus provides a possible model of creation motivated by love.

6. Human novelists may come to love their characters, at least in the sense of coming to feel deeply involved with them and caring how their individual stories will work out. But loving a character is not the same as giving them an easy time within the story, since characters who meet with little or no adversity may have little opportunity to grow and develop in interesting ways.

7. Writing a fictional tale (especially one set in a wholly fictional universe) is possibly the closest human analogy we have to creation ex nihilo (out of nothing), as opposed to constructing an elaborate machine, say, out of pre-existent materials (although human storytelling isn't strictly creation out of nothing, since even the most ingenious storyteller has to rely on his or her experiences for raw material).

8. The authorial model of creation provides a potentially helpful model of how divine action differs in kind from human action (or other kinds of action within the created order), so that God is not made to appear to be just one actor alongside others.

This last point may be illustrated through the following snatch of imaginary dialogue:

> 'I say, Holmes, who do you think is responsible for those vile murders last week?'
> 'Elementary, my dear Watson; it's clearly that scoundrel Conan Doyle. He's the one writing this story, after all!'[11]

In one sense, Holmes's reply is perfectly correct. If Sir Arthur Conan Doyle had penned such a story, then he could indeed be said to have been the person who planned the series of vile murders and ensured that they were executed. Had Conan Doyle decided otherwise, they would not have taken place. On the other hand, Holmes probably hasn't answered the question Watson intended to ask,

---

[11] Eric Eve, Section 9.2 of 'Dialog: A Way Forward', p. 203.

and Holmes could have given a very different kind of answer had he explained that the series of vile murders had been masterminded by Professor Moriarty to keep him (Holmes) distracted from some even more dastardly deed Moriarty was plotting. On this scenario, both Moriarty and Conan Doyle could be said to be responsible for the vile murders, but their actions are of a totally different order. Conan Doyle is not just another actor alongside Moriarty, as, say, Jack the Ripper might be. There is clearly some kind of relationship between the actions and agency of Conan Doyle and Professor Moriarty, but it is quite complex to describe. For example, whereas Moriarty's actions are morally reprehensible, it is far from clear that Conan Doyle's actions can be so described. Be that as it may, Conan Doyle's actions and Professor Moriarty's actions are not competing explanations for the same series of events as if the truth of one implied the falsehood of the other.

The analogy of creation as storytelling thus offers a rather more fruitful model of divine action (as something wholly different in kind from human action or natural causation) than a clockmaker analogy can (in which divine action and natural causation can all too easily appear to be competing explanations for the same event). The Holmes and Watson example also suggests a further point: to provide what Watson would have regarded as a satisfactory answer to his question, Holmes would need to have replied in terms of Professor Moriarty's schemes. Events, people, and actions within a well-constructed narrative need to make sense to the characters within that narrative (or at least, need to be explicable in principle to the characters within that narrative) without recourse to the Author as explanatory category. A well-constructed narrative should make sense on its own terms (however much it may also be legitimate to ask about authorial design). How this may apply to the analogy of creation as storytelling is one of the issues we shall now go on to explore.

2.2.3 Implications and Constraints

We have sketched out some of the main implications of the Storytelling Model of Creation. Some further potential implications arise from the constraints under which authors often work. We are not concerned with such real-world constraints as the need to earn a living, find a publisher, and attract readers, but rather with the artistic constraints inherent in composing a well-constructed narrative as opposed to 'a tale told by an idiot, full of sound and fury, signifying nothing'.[12] Authors *can* do anything they wish in their creations, but to produce worthwhile narratives, they need to respect certain constraints, even while being free to choose many of the constraints they will respect (which will in part be

---

[12] Shakespeare, *Macbeth*, Act V Scene 5.

dictated by genre). Quite apart from any worries about critical reception, an author who is creating a story for the love of it will presumably want to do the best job of it he or she can, which is likely to involve accepting certain self-imposed constraints.

We touched on one of these earlier. The story world and the events and actions that take place within it broadly need to make sense to the characters within the story. This does not, of course, mean that the characters need to be omniscient or that they understand everything or that there cannot be at least an element of mystery (indeed a degree of ignorance and misunderstanding may be essential to the plot), but it does mean that the world in which they operate is sufficiently stable, coherent, and predictable to allow them to plan and act (otherwise they would have no freedom of action at all). If Sally puts the kettle on at some point in the story, the water in the kettle had better boil and not freeze, or if normal expectations are frustrated, there had better be an explanation that makes sense within the story world. (There may, for instance, be an interruption to the gas supply in Sally's apartment so that the kettle never gets a chance to boil and the temperature in the flat falls to sub-zero temperatures in a harsh winter freeze.)

To be sure, authors can sometimes resort to coincidence as a plot device, and this can be legitimate; coincidences do happen, and even highly improbable events sometimes do occur, but over-reliance on coincidence is likely to look like lazy plotting and poor storytelling. In general, a story is likely to be more artistically satisfactory if everything that happens makes sense on its own terms in accordance with the narrative logic both of the world in which it takes place and the psychology of its characters. Sally's kettle should not suddenly turn into a toaster, and neither should Sally suddenly remove all her clothes and jump out of the window for no apparent reason.

That is not at all to say that good stories must conform to current scientific theories about the universe. Science fiction abounds in tales involving faster-than-light travel that current scientific theory rules out, but that doesn't stop Science fiction authors writing perfectly acceptable space opera. It can, of course, be justly objected that faster-than-light travel is regarded as entirely possible by the characters within the narrative, so that the logic of the story world is not thereby violated, but one could write a perfectly good story of interstellar travel written in the near future in which all the characters share our current understanding that one cannot travel faster than the speed of light apart from the sole daring pioneer who invents the first working FTL drive.

Likewise, it's perfectly possible to write perfectly good stories involving magic, telepathy, clairvoyance, ghosts, and other such paranormal phenomena that much modern science would exclude, just as it's perfectly possible to write a coherent novel involving God, angels, demons, and miracle-working saints, and for both such stories to be set in a world much like our own without straining the willing suspension of disbelief that readers might bring to such tales. Moreover, one can set a fantasy epic in an imaginary world in which magic is accepted as part of the normal fabric of life. But even then, the magical, paranormal, or supernatural elements must appear relatively unusual if they are to have the desired impact, and it makes for better storytelling if they work within the constraints of some kind of narrative logic. If everything can be solved with a flick of the hero's wand, there is no story to be told. Had Gandalf been able to teleport the One Ring to Mount Doom in Chapter One of *The Fellowship of the Ring*, there would have been little need for the rest of the trilogy. Conversely, had Gandalf and Sauron both been made arbitrarily powerful, their contest could quickly have descended into the magical equivalent of all-out nuclear war, dissolving Middle-Earth into chaos.

A skilful storyteller also needs to accept constraints in the portrayal of character. Fictional characters can be complex; they can appear exceptional, odd, or eccentric; they can develop in unexpected ways; but they cannot be pushed around arbitrarily by an author who respects the integrity of his or her creation. Gandalf cannot suddenly be made to commit adultery with Galadriel nor can Sherlock Holmes suddenly decide to seize the French throne and set up a royal harem in Paris. Indeed, authors often find that their characters start to develop a life of their own and resist being pushed around at authorial whim. The novelist and theologian Dorothy L. Sayers, for example, discusses how novelists and dramatists should ideally respect the integrity of their creations in terms of both character and plot, and how such respect constitutes love for what they create.[13] This points to the possibility of self-restraint on the apart of the Divine Author. While God could determine everything that happens, including the thoughts and actions of all God's creatures (which would imply a theistic model we might call Theological Determinism), God's respect for the integrity of God's creation can be seen as imposing a voluntary constraint on the extent to which God does so. While God could in principle control what only appears to be human freedom, God leaves space for genuine freedom (implying a model we might call Free Will Theism). The discussion here assumes some form of Free Will Theism, but readers should note that there are also varieties of theistic belief that are closer to Theological Determinism (in which the difficulties of the authorial model of divine-human interaction may appear less acute).

---

[13] Sayers, *Mind*, pp. 50–62.

The precise implications of all this for our authorial model of divine creation and divine action may not be immediately apparent. The analogy does not of itself rule out the possibility of miracle, for it does not tell us precisely what constraints God may decide to work within, and in any case one should not be too quick to push the authorship analogy too far. What the foregoing discussion does, however, suggest is that a monotheistic God who is all-powerful, all-knowing, and all-loving could well have reasons for accepting constraints on the way God exercises God's omnipotence, in the interests of preserving the coherence and integrity of God's creation. It further suggests the kinds of constraints these could be. But before applying this storytelling analogy to the question of miracle, we should first review some of its limitations.

2.2.4 Limitations of the Narrative Model

One major limitation of our narrative model that will occur to many people is the one already alluded to, namely that we are not imaginary characters living in a fictitious narrative but real people living in a real, material universe and exercising real agency. This can be partly mitigated by pointing to the difficulty of defining 'real' in a non-circular fashion, especially in a context where there is nothing more 'real' to contrast it with. From the perspective of characters in a story, they and their world *are* fully real, and if characters in the narrative began questioning their reality, one might wonder what they could point to as truly real by contrast. If the answer is the author and the author's world, then that might chime with religious traditions that regard God and Heaven as more fully real than our current earthly existence. Even without appealing to this line of thought, it could be argued that since the main purpose of the analogy is to model divine action in the world, it works well enough for that purpose, and maybe as well as any analogy can. After all, we can never be external observers watching God at work in creation and observing both God's perspective and creation's perspective in the way we can consider a human author's perspective and the perspective of characters within the narrative. Thus, we can only use limited analogies to try to grasp something we can never directly perceive.

If this mitigation fails fully to satisfy, it may be because when we insist that *we* are real, and not just characters in a story, part of what we mean is that we are experiencing subjects with an inner life in a way that characters in a story are not. It may, of course, be replied that stories often narrate the inner life of their characters, and that part of the power of a good story is that it presents its characters as subjects of experience with which we can empathize, just as we can empathize with our fellow human beings without directly experiencing their inner life. We might regard this as part of the willing suspension of disbelief that enables us to become engrossed in a good story. For most purposes we could apply the same willing suspension of disbelief to allow us to work with an analogy that is admittedly imperfect but may nevertheless be the best we have.

It is also worth pointing out that some narratives (such as histories and biographies) *do* concern real people with real agency and real subjectivity (or people who had such agency and subjectivity while they were alive). To be sure, authors of such non-fictional narratives are not creating in the way novelists create, but they may nevertheless employ many of the same narrative techniques. Biographical and historical narratives are ontologically distinct from the people, events, and experiences they purport to narrate, but they may be the only means we have of getting to know and understand the people, events, and experiences they narrate, so that even when we regard Napoleon Bonaparte or Abraham Lincoln or Ludwig van Beethoven as fully real people, the Bonaparte, Lincoln, or Beethoven we get to know are characters in someone else's narratives about them. To some extent, even the people we know and encounter personally become known to us at least in part through the stories they tell us about themselves and the narratives we construct about them.

Moreover, while the narrative model raises questions about human agency and freewill, such questions are hardly peculiar to the narrative model. Such questions are just as troublesome in any monotheistic system that ascribes full sovereignty to God, the workings of providence, or indeed in any fully deterministic account of nature. This doesn't make the questions go away; they may still represent limitations of the model; but they are limitations of any human attempt to understand the totality of existence, and so do not select against the narrative model.

A more troublesome question is how well the narrative model can accommodate the relationship between God and human beings, not least in regard to worship and prayer (the latter being particularly germane to our wider topic given that miracles may often be regarded as answers to prayer). While one can certainly write a story in which characters pray and worship, such prayer and worship would normally be directed to God (or whatever other supernatural being or beings were appropriate to the story world in question). To write a novel in which the characters pray to the novel's author would feel distinctly odd. (Could one imagine Sherlock Holmes praying to Sir Arthur Conan Doyle?)

Part of the problem here may be the felt inappropriateness of praying to anyone who is less than God. Having Holmes say, 'I will ask Conan Doyle to tell me who committed those vile murders' would feel less odd than having him say, 'I will pray to Conan Doyle to reveal the perpetrator of the vile murders to me', so the latter *may* represent a fairer analogy here. But even the former statement would be odd, unless, perhaps, Conan Doyle had included himself as a character in the story so that Holmes could visit him to make his enquiry; but then it would be the fictional Conan Doyle within the narrative Holmes was asking, not Conan Doyle the author. At a stretch, one might imagine Holmes picking up the telephone to speak to the author Conan Doyle who was otherwise external to the story world, and since it would be the real Conan Doyle who wrote the dialogue, the fictional Conan Doyle on the other end of the phone line would be speaking the real Conan Doyle's words, so in a sense Holmes would be conversing with the author of the story, but it would be an odd story. It would certainly be possible to write a story in which one or more characters petition the author and the author takes their requests into account in what follows in the story, but many readers might feel it contrived, insofar as both the character's requests and the authorial responses to the requests would have been penned by the author.

Many of these problems stem from the difficulty of reconciling a first-person perspective (that of a character within a novel or a human being within our universe) with a third-person perspective (that of an external observer considering the relation between author and story or that of an external observer considering the relation between God and creation), coupled with the fact that while we can occupy the perspective of external observers in the case of author and novel, we can't do so in the case of God and creation. Moreover, while characters in a novel might well live in a story world in which authors write novels (and can be observed doing so), so that the characters could be presented as reasoning from the analogy of novelists and novels to their own situation as characters in a novel, we do not live in a world in which gods create other worlds (and can be observed doing so). This is a limitation of *any* model of creation and divine action, but it is still a limitation.

Other issues concern the nature of world building. A human author can usually take basic physics and the like for granted and doesn't need to oversee everything from the subatomic to the cosmic level. Moreover, our scientific understanding of nature is not just a narrative but an interlocking set of mathematically based laws that can't be arbitrarily tweaked. Here it might be helpful to complement the authorial model with one of musical composition in a given genre, such as western classical music of the tonal period, in which scales, intervals, and harmonics are dependent on underlying mathematical ratios. Such music can contain surprises but has to observe certain conventions if it's to be well crafted and artistically satisfying.

A final limitation of this model is the danger of anthropomorphizing God, that is of comparing God's actions, intentions and designs to those of a human agent when God is something utterly different from a human being. The same problem would attend any analogy by which we try to understand creation and divine action, so it does not select against the proposed narrative model, but it is nonetheless worth bearing in mind. It may be that we are striving to understand something that is beyond our ability to understand; but that doesn't mean we shouldn't do our best to try.

Overall, the narrative model of creation and divine action remains sufficiently serviceable for the purposes of discussing monotheism and miracle, provided we recognize that it inevitably contains some limitations, as any human model of creation and divine action must by virtue of being proposed from a limited human perspective. (We can't stand outside the system to observe God at work.) While human authors can exercise only relative creativity to produce a simulation of reality, the Divine Author exercises full creativity to produce the real thing. A human author may be said to breathe life into his characters; the Divine Author really does so.

2.3 Miracle and Narrative

2.3.1 Miracles as Authorial Actions

On the storytelling analogy, miracles present no special problem in terms of the divine action required, since everything that happens within a story happens by authorial fiat. A miraculous happening does not differ in that respect from a normal, mundane one. As an author, I can just as easily write, 'Sally poured the water out of the kettle and found that it had mysteriously turned into wine' as 'Sally turned poured the water out of kettle and made herself a cup of tea'.

This example nevertheless raises a couple of questions. The first is, although I *can* write the first sentence, is it something I'd choose to if I were the competent author of a coherent story? The second is, would the first sentence in fact indicate that a miracle had taken place (within the story world) or might it just be that Sally's husband John had just played a prank on her by emptying the kettle and refilling it with wine while Sally was out of the room? We'll return to the second question later; for now, we'll concentrate on the first.

In Section 2.2.3, we suggested that authors need to accept some constraints if they are to produce a coherent narrative depicting a story world that is sufficiently stable and coherent for its characters to act meaningfully. If Sally could never be sure whether what came out of her kettle would be water, wine, nitric acid, a poisonous snake, or a mischievous djinn, it is hard to see how she could have survived in her story world long enough to learn how to use a kettle. Of course, one might write a coherent story about a magic kettle that acted in such unpredictable ways, but it would surely have to be the exception rather than the rule. A world in which every object behaved in arbitrary and unpredictable ways would be a meaningless chaos that might function in narrative only as a cautionary tale about the arbitrary use of limitless power.[14] Moreover, for an event to strike either the reader or characters within the story as miraculous, it must presumably be surprising and exceptional. An attempt to write a story in which miracles were as common as spam emails would be self-defeating.

This does not rule out the possibility of miracle. As has already been discussed, a narrative or story world can always accommodate some exceptional events, although the fewer and less spectacular they are the less strain is likely to be placed on the coherence of the narrative. Having the occasional character healed by no apparent medical means, or even perhaps the occasional character brought back to life, might not strain narrative integrity too seriously, especially if such narrative elements are introduced with care. But having World War II won by a series of thunderbolts raining down on the Nazi leadership and knocking the entire Luftwaffe out of the sky would probably strike most readers as a kludgy deus ex machina. A world in which such things happened would not seem to be one in which human action counted for much.

Yet while this might explain why it could be coherent for someone to believe that God could intervene to cure their Aunt Sally of cancer despite God's not having intervened to prevent the Holocaust, it does not tell us whether miracles occur at all or, if so, what scale or frequency of miracles might be possible without threatening the coherence of the world in which we live or compromising God's larger design. Indeed, it's hard to see how this could be reasonably guesstimated, let alone determined by any kind of abstract reasoning or application of the authorial analogy. The most we can do is to offer a few tentative pointers.

The first is that, on the one hand, unlike human authors, God is not constrained by the need to please potential critics. On a monotheistic view of God, God has no peers who can complain that God's work is inartistic because it resorts to too many implausible plot devices, and if we humans try to set ourselves up as the equivalent of literary critics of the divine narrative, God could very well take the view (a) that human beings don't know the full story and so are in no position to judge and (b) that if the clay has no just reason to complain to the potter (Romans 9:19-21), then neither does the character to the author.

The second is that, on the other hand, authors are normally constrained by their choice of genre, so that what is allowable in a text will vary vastly according to whether the text in question is, say, a physics textbook or a work of speculative fiction. But this, of course, is of no help unless we already know what the genre of the text is. If we start from the assumption that the world is a physics textbook (a reasonable thing for physicists to do when they are

---

[14] H. G. Wells's short story. 'The Man Who Could Work Miracles' in his *Tales of the Unexpected*, pp. 110–28, might be a case in point.

working qua physicists), then everything must have a rational explanation and miracles are excluded. If, on the other hand, we think the narrative we inhabit is more akin to something written in a fantasy genre, then all sorts of things will seem possible. It may be that we suppose the truth lies between the two, and that the best analogy to the sort of narrative we inhabit is a 'realistic narrative', but that of course begs the question of what counts as realistic, which in practice is often influenced by both personal experience and cultural perspective.

Sayers discusses the issue of miracle within realistic narratives and concludes that 'it is necessary that God should act in conformity with His own character. The study of our analogy will perhaps lead us to believe that God will be chary of indulging in irrelevant miracle, and will only use it when it is an integral part of the story.'[15] This is helpful but leaves open the question how we are to judge when a miracle is relevant and integral to the story.

At this point we may tentatively conclude that on the narrative model miracles are possible, but easier to accommodate if they are relatively infrequent and relatively small-scale. But this conclusion presupposes that we have a clear idea of what we mean by 'miracle', so our next task will be to attempt to clarify this by discussing miracles as stories (and often, as stories linked to other stories).

2.3.2 Miracle as Story

It may seem trivial to say that accounts of individual miracles come to us in the form of stories if they are to convey anything more than a bare summary such as 'Jesus healed many people' or 'Moses and Aaron performed many signs at the time of the exodus'. But the important point is that it is only the story (and the context that it provides) that indicates whether what is being described is a miracle as opposed to (say) a completely mundane event, a striking coincidence, a conjuring trick, or an inexplicably bizarre occurrence with no apparent meaning at all. Merely labelling something a miracle doesn't make it so.

So, for example, David Basinger correctly draws attention to the importance of context in judging whether something is to count as a miracle.[16] Kenneth Woodward similarly emphasizes the essentially contextualized storied nature of miracles.[17] It is narrative that provides this context. The essentially narrative aspect of miracles is also emphasized by Ruben Zimmerman, whose work contains a helpful discussion of what constitutes the genre 'miracle story'. Whereas Zimmerman's discussion is focused on the Gospel miracle stories,

---

[15] Sayers, *Mind*, pp. 62–67.
[16] Basinger, 'What Is a Miracle?', p. 22, correctly draws attention to the importance of context in judging whether something is to count as a miracle. It is narrative that provides this context.
[17] Woodward, *Book of Miracles*, pp. 19, 22–23, 383.

his definition could be adapted to cover monotheistic miracles more generally. Slightly paraphrased and generalised, it includes 'factual narration' (in the sense of a history-like account of a series of events purporting to have actually occurred) of observable but seemingly inexplicable changes explicitly or implicitly attributed to divine action that astound the percipients with the aim of evoking an appropriate faith response.[18]

So, for example, if someone were to write, 'A miracle occurred yesterday: Sally boiled the kettle and made herself a cup of tea', most readers would assume that 'miracle' was being used ironically to comment on Sally's lack of domestic skills. If, on the other hand, we return to the story in which Sally puts a kettle of water on to boil and returns from a visit to the bathroom to find the kettle full of wine, we should still want further details before deciding whether the story purports to narrate a miracle.

To judge the significance of wine replacing the water in Sally's kettle, we'd want to know the answers to several questions. Was Sally alone in her flat during her visit to the bathroom? If not, can we be sure that the substitution wasn't made by her husband either to play a prank or an ill-advised attempt to make mulled wine? If her husband denies tampering with the kettle, is he to be believed or not? If Sally was apparently alone in the flat, could there nevertheless have been an intruder? Did Sally verify that what she took to be wine when she poured it from the kettle actually was wine (by smelling and tasting it), or could its wine-like appearance be due to contamination in the water supply or some residue in the kettle?

Even supposing the story can reassure us on all those points, we would still need further context to decide whether what was being described was a *miracle*. If the story establishes Sally as a hard-line atheist whose faith in the non-existence of God remains robustly unshaken by this water into wine incident and no one else in the story attaches any religious significance to it whatsoever, then what has been narrated would just be a bizarre anomaly; it would be hard to see it as a *miracle*, since nothing of divine significance would have been conveyed. If the incident occurred within a wider narrative in which Sally's neighbours were a coven of novice witches practising various spells, one might instead read it as a kind of sorcerer's apprentice tale; the witches were trying to turn a jug of water into vintage claret for their own consumption, but the spell went awry and worked on Sally's kettle instead; the story is then about magic, not miracle. If, however, the story tells us that Sally had just been reading the account of the Wedding at Cana in John 2:1-12, that she was facing a crisis that

---

[18] See Zimmerman's contribution to the 'Dialog – A Way Forward', section of Twelftree, *Nature Miracles*, 207–12, and his 'Re-Counting the Impossible', pp. 107–27 (here pp. 109–20).

required a potentially life-changing decision, and that she'd just been praying for a sign, one would be more inclined to read the story as purporting to narrate a miracle.

Conversely, would we necessarily decide that no miracle had occurred if the story gave us a natural explanation for the wine in the kettle? Suppose that on the scenario in which Sally prays for a sign, her absent-minded husband John goes into the kitchen to pour himself a glass of wine but pours the wine into the kettle instead and then promptly forgets all about it. If Sally then takes the apparent water-into-wine miracle as a sign and, as a result, makes a life-changing decision that works out well according to some plausible divine plan (e.g., she retrains as a medic and ends up discovering a breakthrough cure for cancer that saves millions of lives), has a miracle occurred or not? Could one not say that God had used John's absentmindedness to give Sally a nudge with spectacularly beneficial results?

Consider a parallel pair of cases. Suppose that Sally's husband John has been diagnosed with incurable cancer, and he's given only six months to live. In the first case, Sally prays for John's recovery, and he recovers against all medical expectation. In the second, Sally and John are told of an experimental cure available in another country that could save John, but will cost a vast sum of money they can't afford. Sally buys the only lottery ticket she ever buys in her life, prays for the money, and wins just enough money to pay for John's treatment, which turns out to be successful. Many people would regard the first case as miraculous, but what about the second? Is it a miracle or just a huge coincidence?

At this point we should pause to ask a logically prior question. When we ask whether something is a miracle or not, who is to be the judge of the answer? Are we asking whether we as readers of the story either do or should regard it as narrating it as a miracle, or whether the narrator intends it to be understood as a miracle, or whether it's a miracle in God's eyes, or whether Sally regards it as a miracle, or John does, or the people they tell about it? While it is perfectly possible that the answers from all these different perspectives may align, there is no guarantee that they will all do so in every case.

The question whether God might intend any of the scenarios described here as miracles is probably unanswerable apart from how the various humans involved understand them. What God intends is unknowable apart from what God chooses to reveal, and if no one else understands a given event as being miraculous, then no miraculous intention has been revealed. What the narrator intends can fairly be inferred by the way he or she tells the story, although the richer and more detailed the story is and the more it interacts with other stories, the more secure such inference is likely to be. For example, if one of the stories about Sally and John occurs in an anthology of modern miracle stories, or an extended narrative featuring Sally as a devout protagonist frequently experiencing the action of divine grace in her life, the kettle incident or the cancer-cure account is more likely to be understood as intended to be a miracle story than if it occurs in a wider narrative featuring Sally as a robustly unbelieving protagonist who otherwise never encounters anything remotely miraculous and the tone of the narrative shares Sally's uncompromising scepticism. What Sally, John, and various readers take the event to be will also depend on Sally, John, and the various readers.

That is not to say that Sally, John, and the various readers are free to make purely arbitrary decisions on whether or not a miracle has occurred. This may partly depend on such temperamental and intellectual factors as their varying degrees of credulity, scepticism, or critical acumen, which may in turn depend on their individual life stories, but it will also depend on their ability to conceive and weigh up competing narratives. In the case of the wine-in-kettle story, I can always come up with a competing narrative in which a master-burglar scaled the wall, climbed in through Sally's kitchen window, and replaced the water in the kettle with vintage claret in order to win a bet, or in which a junior ensign about the Starship Enterprise on one of its time-travelling jaunts beamed up Sally's kettle, refilled it with wine, and beamed it back down again just to amuse himself with the transporter during an otherwise boring watch. The question is then whether anyone will find such competing narratives more or less plausible than one in which God turned the water into wine to give Sally a sign.

2.3.3 Fact or Fiction?

This discussion has so far proceeded with little regard to whether (and if so in what sense) the narratives are true, since the aim has been to clarify what might count as a miracle. For that purpose, much the same considerations apply whether the story we are reading purports to be fact or fiction. To be sure, biographies should not be read in the same way as novels, but both are narrative genres that contain quite a bit in common, and in deciding whether the wine-in-kettle or cancer-recovery account is meant to be read as a miracle (our judgement of the narrator's intention) we probably work with much the same considerations in each case, except that in the case of an account that purports to be factual, we can and probably often do bring in a much wider context (potentially that of our entire set of real world experience, knowledge and beliefs) than we are likely to do in the case of an avowedly fictitious tale, where we may be more inclined to take our cues from the way things work in the story world (especially when we perceive this to be deliberately different from our own world). But whether something counts as a miracle story is separate from the question of what actually happened or whether it is intended to be taken as fact or fiction.

Clearly, though, when an account purports to be factual (or at least, in some sense true, which may not necessarily be the same thing), additional considerations come into play. The first, and most obvious, is that we are usually no longer willing to accord such accounts the kind of willing suspension of disbelief that attends our reading of fiction. I say 'usually' because if the story coheres strongly with our existing religious beliefs and comes from what we take to be an unimpeachably reliable source, there may be no disbelief to suspend, and far from making us more cautious or sceptical, our existing beliefs may cause us to become more credulous. Otherwise, however, we are likely to be more cautious about accounts of alleged miracles, questioning the reliability of the narrator and probing the possibility of alternative explanations. Quite apart from anything else, there is more at stake in evaluating the truth claims of miracle stories that purport to be factual than in evaluating the narrative function of avowedly fictional ones.

The second, and subtler, difference is that miracle stories that purport to be true introduce additional layers. On a model of miracle working that likens divine action to authorial action, every real-world miracle story involves at least two narrators: God as divine Author who brings the miracle about and at least one human narrator (in practice there may be several) who shapes what has happened into a narrative form that can be humanly received as a miracle story. This remains the case even if the person who experiences the miracle never relates it to anyone else, for in order to first experience and then remember the event as a miracle, the person experiencing it must shape it into a narrative form that makes sense of it as a miracle (as opposed, say, to a purely natural occurrence, a freak accident of nature, a bizarre random coincidence, a conjuring trick, a deliberate deceit, or a piece of magic). For something to take shape as a miracle story doesn't require that the shaping be done by the eyewitness or eyewitnesses of the events in question, it could instead occur in the reception and reshaping of accounts by the person or persons to whom the eyewitnesses report their experiences (e.g., in the Sally and John stories, it could in principle be John who interprets Sally's experiences as miraculous, despite Sally having come to no such conclusion herself). But wherever the shaping occurs, the true miracle takes place at the intersection of the divine and human narratives, that is, where the Divine Author's narrative action is understood as miraculous by one or more human narrators.

Two more points should now be noted in passing. The first is that to talk of the Divine Author's narrative action is not to talk of God as intending something as miraculous in the sense of God regarding it as odd, exceptional, or surprising (as if God could be surprised by what God does), but rather as the Author narrating something that characters in the narrative regard as odd, exceptional, or surprising (which may well be how God intends them to perceive it, although that goes beyond what we can strictly know). The second is that once miracles become a matter of human narration, as they much inevitably do to become knowable as miracles, their truth or falsity may not always be a matter of straightforward binary opposition. There may be some miracle stories some or many people judge to be simply false (on the grounds either that the events they purport to describe never happened or that they weren't miraculous) and some that at least some people judge to be entirely true (because they are foundational to their religious tradition or were convincingly experienced by the people making the judgement or have been narrated by a trustworthy source), but they may well be others that are judged to have been embellished, or to have grown in the telling, or to have been interpretatively shaped, while nevertheless containing a core of factual and perhaps also theological or religious truth.[19]

2.3.4 The Function of Miracle Stories

We should also briefly consider whether enquiring about the factual truth of miracle stories risks missing their point. Ruben Zimmerman, for example, argues that the whole point of miracle stories is to generate an irresolvable tension between the factual manner of their narration and the impossibility of what they narrate, so that the reader or hearer is confronted with the power of a God who breaks through all norms, thereby challenging the accepted order of the world. By so doing, miracle stories may change reality. The recounting of such stories within a given faith community may thus in part be constitutive of that faith community.[20]

One might also view miracle stories as primarily having theological, religious, and/or allegorical functions independent of their factual accuracy. Thus, for example, the Gospel story of Jesus stilling the storm (Mark 4:35-41, on which see later) conveys the Christological point that Jesus acts in a unique way as an agent of the divine, while his healings of the deaf and blind in Mark highlight his difficulties in opening the ears and eyes of his disciples.[21] So also

---

[19] See Eve, 'Growth', pp. 66–85.
[20] Zimmerman, 'Re-Counting the Impossible'; cf. Crossley, 'The Nature Miracles as Pure Myth', pp. 86–106.
[21] See further Eve, *Healer*, pp. 104–12.

in Matthew's Gospel the stories of the Stilling of the Storm and the Walking on the Sea are nudged in the direction of allegories about discipleship and faith, in which the disciple's storm-tossed boat may be seen as a figure of the church assailed by tribulations.

It is clearly important to consider the function and genre of miracle stories before rushing to debate their historical veracity, and of course one may judge differently in different cases. There may well be miracle stories that appear so fanciful (or in so fanciful a context) that one may reasonably doubt whether anyone was ever intended to take them literally. On the other hand, since something would hardly count as a miracle story if it did not have some religious significance, that a miracle story conveys a religious message does not of itself discount its ostensible claim to be factual. So, for example, while the Gospel miracle stories clearly intend to say something about the identity of Jesus of Nazareth, the nature of the truth claim they are making will likely feel rather different if they are all seen as lacking historical foundation. To put it another way, one function of miracle stories can be to legitimate or otherwise support the belief system in which they occur, which then inevitably raises questions about their historical veracity.

We shall return to the questions of how miracle stories may be evaluated and whether miracles ever in fact happen in the final section, but we should first look at some examples of accounts that illustrate miracles as a narrative category.

3 Examples of Miracles

3.1 Introduction

We have argued that miracle is first and foremost a narrative category, insofar as it is the way an event is narrated that identifies it as a miracle. The context of the event, provided by the story in which it is embedded, often together with related stories and background beliefs, plays a vital part in guiding our interpretation of it as a miracle. In this section, we shall illustrate this by sampling miracle stories from monotheistic religions. We shall begin with Jewish miracles narrated within the Old Testament/Hebrew Bible and Second Temple Judaism (represented by the first-century Jewish historian Josephus). We shall then look at some miracles narrated in the New Testament, as well as a small sample of modern Christian miracle stories. We shall finally take a brief look at a couple of Qu'ranic miracle stories. The point will be not to judge the truth or falsity of the stories but to observe how they fit with the narrative model.

3.2 Miracles in Jewish Scripture
3.2.1 Crossing the Red Sea

The bulk of the miracle stories in the Hebrew Bible occur in relation to the exodus. Of these, one of the most foundational is the crossing of the Red Sea (or 'Sea of Reeds') that is narrated as the climax of Israel's escape from Egypt in Exodus 14. Following a series of ten plagues, the Pharaoh of Egypt finally allows Israel to depart, but then changes his mind (because God hardens his heart) and sends his army in pursuit. The Israelites panic, but Moses promises that God will deliver them, and God instructs Moses to stretch out his hand over the sea. When Moses does so, God sends an east wind to drive back the water (Exod. 14:21) so that the Israelites can cross the sea as if walking on dry land, between two walls of water (Exod. 14:22). The Israelites thus reach the other side in safety, but when the Egyptian army attempts to pursue them, God causes their chariot wheels to clog and when Moses stretches his hand out over the sea a second time, the waters return to their normal depth, drowning the Egyptians and allowing the Israelites to complete their escape.

The biblical narrative makes it clear that a miracle is being narrated, not least because of actions directly ascribed to God, but also because of the wider context. In the preceding chapters God has called Moses to lead his people from slavery in Egypt. Moses has confronted Pharaoh, but Pharaoh has remained stubborn until the tenth and final plague slays the firstborn of Egypt. The plagues have followed a pattern of falling on the Egyptians but sparing the Israelites. By the time we get to the Red Sea crossing, Israel has been established by the narratives as God's people whom God has appointed Moses to lead, and what follows in the Hebrew Bible is largely the story of God's dealings with Israel. But the story could have been told differently. One can at least imagine a different version penned by a sceptical Egyptian chronicler maintaining either that the Israelite escape was just pure bad luck (from the Egyptian perspective) due to a coincidental confluence of wind and tide, or else that Moses cunningly used his local knowledge of the winds and tides to lead the Egyptians into a trap. From the perspective of this hypothetical Egyptian chronicler, 'God sent an east wind to drive back the water' might become 'an east wind drove back the water' (which is all that an observer would have seen) and 'God caused their chariot wheels to clog' might become 'our chariots became bogged down in the damp sand'. The crossing of the Red Sea becomes a foundational miracle by virtue of the way in which it is narrated and the wider narrative context in which it is set.

The crossing of the Red Sea also affords a good illustration of the authorial model of divine action. The way in which God orchestrates events to effect

Israel's escape from Egypt resembles the way in which an author might orchestrate events to further the plot of the novel. The frequent notices that Gods hardens the hearts of Pharaoh and the Egyptians in order to manifest God's glory (e.g., Exod. 14:17) may seem disturbing, but are similar in principle to a human author making characters perform the role assigned to them and are not incompatible with those characters acting from motives of their own (e.g., Exod. 14:5).

3.2.2 Miraculous Feedings

Shortly after the Israelites escape at the Red Sea, they complain that they have nothing to eat (Exod. 16:3). God accordingly promises Moses that he will rain 'bread from heaven', which the people are to collect on six days each week and refrain from collecting on the seventh. In addition, quails settle in the camp, allowing the Israelites to eat meat (Exod. 16:13; cf. Num. 11:31-33). Each morning (apart from the seventh) the Israelites discover a flaky substance on the ground left over after the evaporation of the dew (Exod. 16:14). They call this manna; it tastes like wafers baked with honey (Exod. 16:31) and provides their staple diet for the duration of their wilderness wanderings. Attempts to gather more than is needed on each day go awry when the surplus is found to have gone off the following day, unless it is the Sabbath on which no manna is available to be collected.

A different story could have made the finding of the manna and the arrival of the quails purely serendipitous or the result of Moses's canny leadership (exploiting his local knowledge to lead his people under the quails' habitual flight path where it intersected with a clump of tamarisk trees, the likely source of the manna). But that is not the story told here, in which everything occurs according to God's commands in response to the Israelites' complaints (according to the version in Numbers 11, God sends the wind that sends the quails to the Israelite camp, though not with entirely happy results since eating a surfeit of quails makes them ill; cf. Josephus, *Antiquities* 3.24-25). The story is miraculous because the manna appears in sufficient quantity to sustain the whole of Israel throughout their forty-year march (and it would be hard to imagine that Israel constantly remained within walking distance of large numbers of tamarisk trees always in season for dropping manna) and on a weekly cycle that conform to the Sabbath regulations that will form part of the commandments given on Mount Sinai. The story thus emphasizes both God's miraculous provision for his people and their need to depend on it and to maintain their obedience to God, and once again one has a sense of God orchestrating events like the Author of a story.

To the story of miraculous feeding with manna and quails, we may add the curious little story in which Elisha feeds a hundred men with twenty loaves and there is bread left over after they have all eaten (2 Kgs 4:42-44). Of itself, this might not seem all remarkable if we imagine a loaf as being the kind of thing we might purchase at a modern supermarket, but we should probably imagine it as being more on the scale of a large bread roll, a sufficient (but hardly generous) quantity for one meal for one person. This is confirmed by Elisha's servant's complaint that the twenty loaves are insufficient for a hundred people. That divine action is involved is signalled through Elisha telling his servant that the Lord has decreed that everyone will eat and there will be some left, and the narrator subsequently stating that it happened according to the word of the Lord. That this is intended as a miracle story is further implied by the context in which it occurs, a cycle of stories involving the prophets Elijah and Elisha. Earlier in the chapter, Elisha has relieved a widow's poverty through the miraculous multiplication of oil which she can go on to sell (2 Kgs 4:1-7), raised another woman's son from the dead (2 Kgs 4:8-37) and rendered an accidentally poisoned pot of stew edible (2 Kgs 4:38-41), and in the following chapter he will cure the Syrian general Naaman of leprosy (2 Kings 5). The cycle of miracle stories concerning Elisha thus establishes him as a mighty man of God comparable to his immediate predecessor Elijah, of whom a similar cycle of stories is narrated. (The Elijah and Elisha cycles give us a concentration of miracle stories the like of which are not encountered again in the Bible until we come to the Gospels.)

Again, one could imagine versions of these stories that didn't emphasize the miraculous. In the story of the multiplication of oil, Elisha tells the widow to borrow jars from her neighbours to fill from her own single remaining jar of oil. In a non-miraculous version, perhaps Elisha urges the neighbours to donate the oil in the vessels they lend. Perhaps, also, Elisha performed the kiss of life on the other woman's seemingly deceased son, thereby resuscitating him, Elisha's addition of flour to the poisoned stew was just a natural way to neutralize the poison, and Naaman's cure was psychosomatic. (Biblical leprosy was not Hansen's disease, which is what we now mean by leprosy, but some form of skin disease that could plausibly be exacerbated by stress, and we could hypothesize that Naaman calmed down after taking seven dips in the Jordan because he believed this would work.) But these are not the stories 2 Kings narrates, and it is the way 2 Kings narrates them that makes us see them as miracle stories.

3.2.3 Hezekiah's Prayer

2 Kgs 18-19 ‖ Isa. 36–37 narrate the start of the reign of King Hezekiah of Judah, whom the narrator regards as being a rare worthy successor to the great King David in his loyalty and devotion to God. When the Assyrian King Sennacherib sends a large army to invade Judah, Hezekiah at first attempts to buy them off with gold and silver from the temple, but an Assyrian official stands outside the walls of Jerusalem telling its inhabitants not to rely on Hezekiah's promise that their God will deliver them from the Assyrian attack. His speech mocks not only Hezekiah's shortage of cavalrymen but also Hezekiah's God, who is likened to the powerless gods of other lands conquered by Assyria. Hezekiah repairs to the temple dressed in sackcloth and ashes and there encounters the prophet Isaiah who assures the king that God has heard the Assyrian mockery and advises him to pray to the Lord. The Assyrian official subsequently sends Hezekiah a threatening letter that again mocks God's impotence, which Hezekiah takes to the temple to spread before the Lord before uttering his prayer for salvation. Isaiah then sends Hezekiah a message telling him that the Lord has heard his prayer, continuing with an oracle against the Assyrian king spoken in the name of the Lord, and concluding with the promise that the Assyrians will not attack the city because the Lord will defend it. That very night, the Angel of the Lord slays 185,000 Assyrian troops, forcing the Assyrians to withdraw.

A different version of this story could have the Assyrians robbed of victory by a fortuitous outbreak of plague in their camp, but the biblical account sets it in a context in which God responds to the prayer of a faithful king of Judah, speaks through one of Judah's greatest prophets, and acts against an arrogant foe who dare to mock God's name. Given this wider narrative context, what is described here is not a lucky escape but a miraculous deliverance.[22]

3.3 Miracles in Josephus

Josephus was a Jewish historian and apologist for Judaism who flourished in the second half of the first century CE. Having taken part in the Jewish revolt, he went on to write a detailed account of that conflict and then several other works, of which the most germane for our purposes is the *Jewish Antiquities*, a twenty-volume history of the Jewish people from the creation down to the eve of the Jewish War. The first half of the *Antiquities* retells the narratives of the Jewish

---

[22] For further discussions of miracles in the Jewish Scriptures, see Ross, 'Some Notes on Miracle in the Old Testament', pp. 45–60 and Moberly, 'Miracles in the Hebrew Bible', pp. 57–74. For the development of Jewish thought on miracles, see Seeskin, 'Miracles in Jewish Philosophy', pp. 254–70.

Scriptures, including many of the miracle stories they include. This is not the place to review Josephus's treatment of these stories in any detail; a couple of examples will have to suffice.[23]

1 Kgs 13:1-10 tells of a man of God from Judah, who accosts King Jeroboam when the king was offering incense to a golden calf at an altar he had previously set up at Bethel (1 Kgs 12:25-33), which we're meant to understand as an act of idolatry by the breakaway king. The man of God tells Jeroboam that a future Davidic king, Josiah, will defile this altar and then offers Jeroboam a sign that this will take place by foretelling that the altar will be torn down. When Jeroboam stretches out his hand to order the Judean prophet's arrest, the king's hand is withered and the altar collapses. At the king's request, the prophet prays for Jeroboam's hand to be restored, and it duly is.

Josephus relates his version of this story at *Antiquities* 8.243-245, going on to describe how a false prophet then persuades Jeroboam that the man of God from Judah was not a genuine prophet. The false prophet argues that the supposed signs have a natural explanation: Jeroboam's hand had been temporarily numbed by the fatigue of carrying the sacrifice, and the new altar had collapsed under the weight of the items placed on it. Jeroboam accepts these rationalizations. This false prophet is an addition to the biblical narrative, presumably aimed at explaining why Jeroboam persisted in his evil ways despite the sign he'd just been given. He also illustrates Josephus's appreciation of competing narratives; here the Judean prophet and the false prophet give competing explanations for what has taken place, and the renegade king of Israel chooses the one that suits him rather than one that involves faithfulness to the God of Israel.

While most of the miracle stories narrated in the *Antiquities* are retellings of biblical ones, Josephus does include a few post-biblical ones. One is the shower of rain that accompanies the Roman legate Petronius's decision not to carry out Caligula's order to have his statue erected in the temple at Jerusalem (*Antiquities* 18.285). Stated thus baldly, this may not look particularly miraculous; it is the context that makes it so. Josephus emphasizes that this shower came out of a clear blue sky during a prolonged drought. The context implies that the Jews protesting against Caligula's flagrant idolatry have placed themselves in considerable peril by standing up to a Roman legate backed by Roman troops and that Petronius, the legate in question, displays both discernment and moral courage in going against the emperor's orders. When Caligula hears what he's done, he sends a message ordering Petronius to commit suicide, which the legate is only spared from doing by news of Caligula's death. Moreover, Josephus explicitly states that God sent

---

[23] For fuller discussions, see Eve, *Jewish Context*, pp. 24–52; MacRae, 'Miracle in the *Antiquities* of Josephus', pp. 129–47; Novakovic, 'Miracles in Second Temple and Early Rabbinic Judaism', pp. 95–112.

this rain as a sign of support for both Petronius and the Jews. Here again it is the way the event is narrated and the wider narrative context that invites us to see it as miraculous (something seemingly inexplicable attributed to divine action and possessing clear religious significance).

To be sure, in Josephus the miraculous can often shade into the merely providential (providence being one of Josephus's leading theological categories in the *Antiquities*). Moreover, writing for a potentially sceptical Graeco-Roman audience, Josephus will sometimes offer rationalizing explanations for the miracles he recounts and frequently states that his readers can make up their own minds on such matters (*Ant.* 1.108; 2.328; 3.81; 4.158; 10.281; 17.354), but neither feature of Josephus's account is intended to express his own doubt about the miraculous. What Josephus brings to the discussion is rather a recognition that miracles are often in the eye of the perceiver. This does not at all mean that they are not real, but that Josephus recognizes that they need to be viewed from a perspective of belief in God to be perceived as miracles.

3.4 Miracles in the Gospels

3.4.1 Introduction

This is not the place for an extensive discussion of the nature and function of the miracle stories in the Gospels, so in what follows we shall briefly survey four miracle stories taken from the Gospel of Mark to illustrate how their significance depends not only on the details of the individual stories but also on their wider narrative context within Mark's Gospel. We focus on Mark both because of its relatively high concentration of miracle stories and because since Mark is almost certainly the earliest of the four canonical gospels its treatment of Jesus's miracles is foundational for the rest.[24]

3.4.2 The Capernaum Demoniac

The casting out of an evil spirit from the possessed man in the Capernaum synagogue is the first act of power narrated in Mark's Gospel (Mark 1:21-28). If this story appeared in isolation, it might be debatable whether it should be called a miracle. Jesus would hardly have been the only successful Jewish exorcist; indeed, Josephus describes an exorcism he witnessed as if it were simply a matter of employing the correct technique (*Antiquities* 8.45-49).[25] Moreover, there is an abundance of anthropological literature on events indigenously

---

[24] For more extensive treatments of the miracle stories in Mark, see Glasswell, 'The Use of Miracles in the Markan Gospel', pp. 151–62; Twelftree, *Jesus the Miracle Worker*, pp. 55–101; Woodward, *Book of Miracles*, pp. 105–23; Eve, *Healer*, pp. 92–117.

[25] Eve, *Jewish Context*, pp. 326–49 (pp. 339–42 for the Josephus reference).

interpreted as spirit possession and exorcism. In isolation, then, the story of the Capernaum Demoniac could be taken as a story about a powerful healer or spirit-controller, without being labelled as strictly miraculous.

That something more is at stake in Mark's story is suggested by two features in particular: the way in which it emphasizes Jesus's exceptional authority and way the unclean spirits identify Jesus as the Holy One of God who has come to destroy them. Mark emphasizes Jesus's authority both through his teaching (not something one would normally regard as miraculous) and through his power to command the unclean spirits and secure their obedience, which the onlookers clearly regard as sufficiently remarkable for Jesus's fame to spread rapidly.

It is, however, the wider context of this story that invites us to see this as the first of Jesus's miracles in Mark's account. By this stage of his Gospel, Mark has already established that Jesus is the Messiah and Son of God who has come to proclaim the coming of God's Kingdom (Mark 1:1, 11, 14-15), so Jesus has already been established as more than just another prophet-healer-exorcist, and in what follows Jesus will be shown to be a quite remarkable healer-exorcist exercising a quite exceptional degree of authority.

3.4.3 The Healing of the Paralytic

By the time we reach the Healing of the Paralytic at Mark 2:1-12, Jesus has performed several other healings and exorcisms (narrated only in summary) and healed a leper (of which a detailed account is given in Mark 1:40-45). When Jesus returns to Capernaum at Mark 2:1, four people dig through the roof of the house he's speaking in to lower a paralytic down on a stretcher. Jesus at first responds by telling the paralytic that his sins are forgiven. When the scribes in the audience then complain that only God has the authority to forgive sins, Jesus responds by asking whether it is easier to forgive sins or to tell the paralytic to get up and walk, and then, in order to show that the Son of Man has authority on earth to forgive sins, he promptly issues the latter command to the paralytic. The paralytic promptly stands up, picks up his stretcher, and walks off with it, causing everyone else present to cry out in amazement that they have never seen anything like it.

Three features of this narrative signal that something highly unexpected has happened: the astonishment of the onlookers, the instant recovery of the paralytic (whose muscles one might have expected to atrophy had he been in that condition for an extended period), and the implication of Jesus's question that healing the paralytic will be more difficult than forgiving his sins. Quite apart from the wider context in which this story occurs, divine action is introduced into the narrative by the scribes' question: Who other than God can forgive sins? The apparent implication is that Jesus is claiming to act as God.

There are, however, a couple of puzzles here. Jesus does not declare 'I forgive your sins' but 'your sins are forgiven' which, taken in isolation, could be understood as a divine passive meaning 'God forgives your sins', so that Jesus would not be enacting forgiveness on his own authority but announcing God's forgiveness (although that would still raise the question of his authority to do so). But this interpretation is apparently ruled out by Jesus going on talk about the Son of Man having authority on earth to forgive sins, which raises the question, who is 'the Son of Man' and what does the title mean? At this point the first-time reader or hearer of Mark's Gospel may be unsure. The Hebrew idiom underlying 'son of man' can just mean 'human being'. Some scholars have argued that the Aramaic equivalent can also function like the English indefinite pronoun 'one', including its use as an oblique self-reference, in which case Jesus might be saying 'to show that one has authority to forgive sins' meaning 'to show that I have authority to forgive sins'. In the context of the Gospel as a whole, however, it becomes clear that 'the Son of Man' always refers to Jesus and that it ends up as an allusion to the 'one like a son of man' at Dan. 7:13, who is transported to the presence of God by the clouds of heaven to receive everlasting kingship and dominion (Mark 13:26; 14:62). Mark (in common with the other Gospels) thus uses this title to emphasize both Jesus's vulnerable humanity (leading to his death on the cross) and his divine authority. The significance of this miracle story thus only becomes fully apparent when it is understood within the wider context of a Gospel whose significance can in turn only be fully appreciated in relation to the Jewish Scriptures.

3.4.4 The Stilling of the Storm

This dependence on the wider context becomes even more pronounced in the Stilling of the Storm at Mark 4:35-41. By this point in Mark's Gospel, the Healing of the Paralytic has been followed by a series of healing and conflict stories culminating in the Beelzebul Controversy (Mark 3:22-30) in which Jesus is accused of casting out demons by the power of Satan; Jesus's power is not denied but the source of that power is disputed. Jesus's counterargument is that Satan would hardly declare war on himself, so that (at least by implication, 3:29) it is not an evil spirit but the Holy Spirit that empowers Jesus's actions. It may well be that we are thus to understand Jesus's scribal opponents as among those who see without perceiving and hear without understanding (4:12).

In the present scene, Jesus and his disciples board a boat to cross the Sea of Galilee. While Jesus sleeps, a great storm arises and the disciples panic, fearing that they will perish when the boat becomes swamped. When they wake Jesus, he at once rebukes the wind and sea resulting in the immediate cessation of the wind and a dead calm, prompting the disciples to ask, 'Who then is this, that even wind and sea obey him?'

Even taken in isolation this story implies that something stupendous has taken place. Normal human beings don't have the power to still storms with a word of command, and the disciples' question makes plain that this raises the question not just of Jesus's authority but also of his identity. One could imagine a situation in which Jesus speaks a reassuring word to the disciples just as the storm is starting to abate of its own accord, but that's not the story that's told here.[26] The very suddenness with which a dead calm replaces the raging wind and waves tells against it. There's also the wider context of Mark's Gospel, where the strong possibility that Jesus's actions involve divine action has by now been evoked several times.

But it is the Jewish scriptures that provide the clearest answer to the disciples' question, for in those scriptures it is Yahweh the God of Israel who alone commands the wind and sea. Mark's story of the storm echoes the story of the storm stilling in Jonah 1:4-16, in which the prophet Jonah is roused from sleep to pray to God to end a storm (that God has in this case sent). It also evokes Psalm 107:23-30, especially vv. 28-29, in which God stills a storm and the waves of the sea in response to the mariners' cry of distress. More obliquely, it also evokes the crossing of the Red Sea (discussed earlier), partly because the miracle at the Red Sea is paradigmatic for God's mastery over the sea, and partly because Mark's story of the storm is immediately followed by that of the Gerasene demoniac (Mark 5:1-20), which culminates in the drowning of a legion of pigs in the very same sea (recalling the drowning of Pharaoh's army).[27] Given this wider context, there can only be one possible answer to the disciples' 'who is this?' question and hence no doubt that this is a story about divine action.

3.4.5 The Feeding of the Five Thousand

Exodus allusions are surely also intended in Mark's account of the Feeding of the Five Thousand (Mark 6:30-44). On the face it, Mark's feeding story more closely resembles the Elisha feeding story (2 Kings 4:42-44) that we discussed earlier. An exodus allusion may be intended by the way in which Jesus instructs the disciples to get the crowd to sit down in groups of fifty and a hundred (Exod.

---

[26] For the possibility that Mark's story could have grown from some such incident, see Eve, 'Growth', pp. 77–78.

[27] Eve, *Healer*, pp. 153–56. For the point that miracle stories derive their meaning by echoing other events in the same tradition, see Woodward, *Book of Miracles*, pp. 23, 37.

18:21, 25; Deut. 1:15).[28] Such an allusion is further strengthened by the exodus typology that has already been evoked in Mark, and by the proximity of the feeding story to the immediately following account of Jesus's walking on the Sea of Galilee, with the close collocation of the two (sea crossing and miraculous feeding) creating a clearer evocation of the exodus stories than either might in isolation. Once again, context is important, as it is in John 6 where the allusion to the manna miracle in the feeding story is explicitly underlined in the ensuing bread of life discourse.

Without that wider context it would be less clear what this story was narrating. The disciples clearly regard feeding the crowd as problematic, and it would indeed clearly be impossible to satisfy such a large crowd from such meagre resources as five loaves and two fishes. That Jesus looks up to heaven while breaking and blessing the bread perhaps indicates that divine action is involved, but his action resembles that with the bread at the last supper (Mark 14:22) and, indeed, that of any Jewish host at a formal meal, without either implying anything miraculous. We are not told how the feeding is accomplished: Do the five loaves and fishes multiply in some way it is hard to imagine, or, as has often been suggested, do Jesus's actions with the loaves and fishes encourage other people to share what they have brought, with the results described? We are also not told that either the disciples or the crowds reacted with any surprise at what took place (and it's not entirely clear that the disciples understood it; see Mark 8:17-21). If we only had the 2 Kings 4 parallel to go on, we might conclude that Jesus was being depicted as a prophet like Elisha, only more so.

So here again it is the wider context that guides our interpretation of the story as a miracle. As we have seen, by this point in Mark's Gospel, Jesus has already been depicted as performing acts one might regard as peculiar to God alone, and this is about to be reinforced by the immediately ensuing story of Jesus walking on the sea, which functions as a diving epiphany.[29] Moreover, this is not the only story of Jesus feeding a crowd in this way, since Mark will shortly give us the parallel story of Jesus feeding a crowd of 4,000 with 7 loaves. As Oscar Wilde might have said, to feed one crowd from such meagre resources may be down to good fortune; to feed two looks like miracle working.

3.5 Contemporary Miracles

So far, our examples have all been taken from Jewish and Christian antiquity, but accounts of miracles have continued to the present day in far greater profusion that we can even begin to cover here. To give a tiny sample, we

---

[28] Eve, *Healer*, pp. 151–53.   [29] For a detailed treatment, see Heil, *Jesus Walking on the Sea*.

shall employ the substantial collection of contemporary healing miracle accounts in the magisterial work of Craig Keener.[30] Keener's principal aim is to counter scholarly scepticism about the miracles of Jesus by demonstrating that eyewitness accounts of miracles can and do arise, in the context of arguing against western academic anti-supernaturalism as a minority view, which may not be as well founded as its adherents suppose. We can sample only a handful of the accounts Keener cites from around the world.

The first is taken from the Philippines and concerns a thirty-three-year-old woman who was diagnosed with potentially life-threatening heart disease. Her husband proposed selling their house to pay for the surgery that might help her, but the woman told him not to do so as she would just pray. She continued to take her medication for three months, but her breathing got worse, so she decided to abandon her medication and rely on God alone. She then fully recovered and her husband became a Christian believer and subsequently the leader of a Bible school.[31] The point here is not whether one might be able to offer a naturalistic explanation for this course of events, but that when the couple subsequently told Keener what had happened, they presumably intended to tell him about a miracle, and that what makes it a miracle story is the apparent hopelessness of the woman's condition absent appropriate medical intervention coupled with the cure that resulted once she decided to put all her trust in God.

The second is an account from Cuba of a baby who badly burned her hand on a hot iron, leaving her hand peeling and swollen. According to her grandmother's account, the baby's hand was completely healed within a half hour of prayer, leaving no trace of the burn, although no medical intervention had occurred. The grandmother (who shared this story with Keener) was not only a Christian evangelist but also a medical doctor (who would thus be conversant with the severity of burns).[32]

The third comes from the USA. A man returning from a spiritual retreat broke his ankle while checking the oil in his car. The X-ray at a hospital in Missouri revealed a particularly severe fracture that the therapist warned would need several months of therapy. But while the man was kept in overnight at the hospital, he experienced God assuring him that his foot was not broken. After his wife drove him home the following day, the man's doctor sent him to a hospital in Michigan for more X-rays. These showed that no break had taken place, although the X-rays from Missouri still showed it clearly had.

---

[30] Keener, *Miracles*.
[31] Keener, *Miracles*, p. 271. Keener derived his account from interviewing the husband and wife involved.
[32] Keener, *Miracles*, p. 345.

The ankle was blue for a couple of days, but the man had no difficulty walking on it and that Sunday he testified in church how God had healed him.[33]

The fourth relates the raising from the dead of Keener's sister-in-law Thérèse. When she was about two, Thérèse was bitten by a snake and stopped breathing. Her mother ran to an evangelist she believed could help, a journey she estimated took about three hours. No medical assistance was available, so once Thérèse's mother reached the evangelist they could only pray. When they did so, Thérèse began breathing again and was completely recovered by the following day. In adult life she has gone on to do church work. Keener makes the point that although one cannot prove beyond all reasonable doubt that Thérèse had in fact stopped breathing, his mother-in-law came from a culture much more familiar with death at first hand than many in the modern west and would surely have been desperate to detect any signs of life in her daughter, that three hours without oxygen should have caused irreparable brain damage, and that this event occurred within the context of several other apparent miracles.[34]

In each of these cases something extraordinarily unexpected is said to have occurred in a context in which a story of divine action can plausibly be given within a context of theistic belief. That a sceptical counter narrative could also be given is not germane at this juncture, since here the point is to show how modern miracles are also identified by the narrative in which they embedded. If the baby's hand had been spontaneously restored with no reference to prayer, or the traveller's ankle fracture mysteriously healed with no reference to a divine voice or context of religious belief, or Keener's sister-in-law simply recovered from her apparently fatal snake bite after not breathing for three hours for no apparent reason at all, one might loosely speak of 'miracles' in the sense of seemingly inexplicable events, but the context for telling a story of divine action would be lacking.

I have cited only four out of the hundreds of miracle accounts that Keener gives. I narrowed down the field by selecting stories that were more than bare summaries and in which Keener was close to the eyewitness source but even that would have left far too many to be included here.

Woodward's book also contains a discussion of modern miracles. He suggests that most modern miracles are private, typically involving healing but lacking the wider cultural resonance of classical miracle stories with a tendency to trivialize the miraculous by seeing it manifested in God's micromanagement of fortuitous aspects of everyday life. Woodward nonetheless goes on to narrate

---

[33] Keener, *Miracles*, pp. 439–40. Keener received this account from the man's Baptist pastor.
[34] Keener, *Miracles*, pp. 557–58.

some more publicly significant miracles while noting that these are meaningful only within the traditions of the relevant interpretive communities.[35]

3.6 Miracles in Islam

Since this is a book on *monotheism* and *miracle*, at least brief mention should be made of miracles in Islam, though constraints of space will not allow us to explore them in any great depth.

Several of the more notable miracles narrated in the Qu'ran involve figures familiar from the Judaeo-Christian tradition, regarded by the Qu'ran as prophets whose messages are authenticated by signs. For example, Sura 21:51-71 tells how Abraham protested against his people's idolatry by smashing all but one of their idols and sarcastically challenging them to seek answers from the one that remained. In response, the people sentence Abraham to be burnt to death, but God delivered him from the flames (with which compare the similar Jewish account in Pseudo-Philo, *Book of Biblical Antiquities* 6; 32:1). Sura 28 gives an account of the career of Moses, which is similar to that found in the book of Exodus, and at 28:31-32 recounts two of the signs God gave Moses at the burning bush, the rod that transformed into a snake and back and the hand that turned white when Moses slipped it inside his garments (cf. Exod. 4:1-7). At 3:47-49 an angel tells the virgin Mary that the child to be born to her will heal the blind and the leper and raise the dead to life by Allah's will and give a sign from Allah through Jesus making a clay bird and breathing life into it so that it becomes a real bird, again by Allah's will, emphasizing that the miracles are to be performed by Allah to authenticate his prophet rather than by Jesus in his own power (for the last of these miracles cf. *The Inf. Gos. Thom.* 2:1-5). The Qur'an also narrates miracles from Muslim history, including a couple reminiscent of the Hezekiah miracle described earlier: an account of Allah sending birds to pelt an invading army with stones, thereby staving off an attack on Mecca (Sura 105) and Allah sending an army of angels in defence of the Muslim army and making each army appear smaller to the other (thus making the pagans overconfident while encouraging the Muslims – 8:10, 44).[36]

Islamic miracle stories are by no means confined to the Qur'an. In other Islamic literature many miracles are ascribed to Muhammed and, for example, to various Sufi saints, one of the most salient in the former category being Muhammed's night flight to Jerusalem.[37] There is, however, insufficient space to go into these here.

---

[35] Woodward, *Book of Miracles*, pp. 365–82; for the particular points noted in the text, see pp. 365–56, pp. 374–75, p. 383).

[36] Thomas, 'Miracles in Islam', pp. 199–202.

[37] See Woodward, *Book of Miracles*, pp. 173–230, 185–89 for a list of the prophet's miracles; pp. 191–97 for his miraculous night journey.

While the Qur'anic miracles tend to be narrated more succinctly than their biblical equivalents, the same basic pattern appears. The events described are clearly quite out of the ordinary, they further the divine purpose, and divine action is strongly emphasized. The Qur'anic belief that God is directly involved in all events is also consonant with the authorial model of creation and divine action.

3.7 Summary

The foregoing examples have all aimed at illustrating how understanding something as a miracle depends on the narrative in which it is recounted along with the wider context of that narrative (which may often include other narratives to which it is related). That something is intended to be understood as a miracle may be signalled in various ways, from explicit authorial comment to the reactions of the characters involved to allusions to the wider context and to other stories and beliefs. Where alternative narratives suggesting non-miraculous interpretations have been offered, this has not been with the intent of debunking the miracle stories, but rather to illustrate how understanding something as miraculous depends on the way in which it is narrated. The possibility of competing narratives nevertheless leads neatly into our final section, on how the historical (or factual) veracity of miracle stories may be assessed.

4 Assessing Miracles

4.1 Introduction

Narrative models of creation, divine action, and miracle go some way towards addressing the difficulties with the clockmaker analogy (an effectively deistic conception of a God who creates nature as a fully autonomous system and leaves it to run on according to its own principles), but they don't solve everything, and like all analogies they inevitably have their limitations. Not least, the author analogy risks sidestepping the question whether miracles actually can or do occur, and if so, how one is to go about assessing the veracity of individual miracle accounts. Not least, the author analogy might be accused of blurring the distinction between fact and fiction and sitting too lightly on problems that arise in connection with miracles that appear to be physically inexplicable.

This is not the place to settle debates on the possibility of miracle that have been running for centuries, but we should look briefly at how some aspects of the debate may be incorporated into our narrative model. Although this is a step that has been followed many times before, it will be convenient to start with arguments advanced by David Hume.

4.2 Weighing the Evidence

Hume's chapter 'Of Miracles'[38] may not have offered much that was original at the time it was written, and has been since much discussed, defended, and criticized. While it would not be appropriate to replough these furrows in any great depth here, in brief we can say that while Hume's argument can be criticized in detail, he nevertheless has a point, although not one that definitively settles the issue.

Hume starts from the seemingly unobjectionable proposition that 'A wise man, therefore, proportions his belief to his evidence'. He argues that this may result in a certain conclusion when past experience has proved infallible but only to a judgement of probability where it has been less uniform.[39] One can, of course, point out that evidence and experience are not neutral, objective categories, because both terms imply elements of interpretation that Hume's empiricism does not fully allow for, but this does not seriously undermine the point he is making (although it may qualify it). Hume goes on to observe that while we frequently rely on the testimony of others, experience shows us that it is not always reliable. Had Hume been aware of advances in the psychology of memory over the last century or so, he could doubtless have made more of the possibilities of memory distortion, but this would not materially affect his argument.

Where Hume's argument becomes more controversial is where he applies this to the question of miracle:

> A miracle is a violation of the laws of nature; and as a firm and unalterable experience has established these laws, the proof against a miracle, from the very nature of the fact, is as entire as any argument from experience can possibly be imagined ... The plain consequence is (and it is a general maxim worthy of our attention), 'That no testimony is sufficient to establish a miracle unless the testimony be of such a kind, its falsehood would be more miraculous that the fact, which it endeavours to establish;'[40]

There is plenty to quibble with here. First, Hume's definition is not of *miracle* but of *anomaly*, so his argument does not apply to miracles in general, but only to those that involve anomaly. Second, one may question his empiricist account of the establishment of the laws of nature through uniform experience, since one might better characterize it as the forming and testing of theories. Moreover,

---

[38] Hume, *Enquiries*, Section X, pp. 109–31. [39] Hume, *Enquiries*, X.87, pp. 110–11.
[40] Hume, *Enquiries*, X.90–91, pp. 114–16.

since such theories may become modified over time, one might question the claim that human experience either has established or even could establish what the unalterable laws of nature are. Hume overstates his case here. He nevertheless has a point when he concludes that the plausibility or otherwise of a purported miracle needs to be weighed against the plausibility or otherwise of the falsehood of the testimony to that miracle.

That Hume does overstate his case is suggested by some of the examples he gives. He describes Tacitus's and Suetonius's accounts of the healing of a blind man and a lame man by Vespasian in Alexandria as 'one of the best attested miracles in all profane history' but then, having made a solid case for the strength of this testimony, promptly concludes without argument 'that no evidence can well be supposed for so gross and palpable a falsehood'.[41] But how does Hume know that the Roman historians' accounts are false, or does he simply assume what he needs to demonstrate? Hume is here perhaps guilty of confusing miracle with anomaly and failing to see that the events described could have occurred without being anomalous (either through natural means of healing, as Tacitus suggests, or, perhaps, through careful stage-management by the priests of Serapis to boost both their own and the aspiring emperor's legitimacy).[42] He could also be accused of arguing in a circle by excluding the possibility of a genuinely miraculous healing a priori, regardless of the strength of the testimony.

Hume further imagines a hypothetical example, in which all competent historians of England agree that Queen Elizabeth I died on 1 January 1600, that her death was witnessed by her physicians and her court, that her successor was proclaimed by parliament, but that after being interred for a month she reappeared alive and well and resumed the throne for a further three years. Even granting that pretending her death in such a way would be both pointless and extremely difficult to pull off, Hume robustly states that he would still prefer such a bizarre conspiracy theory over crediting the violation of the laws of nature that would result from her in fact rising from the dead, on the basis 'that the knavery and folly of men are such current phenomena'.[43] Hume may be entitled to his judgement here, but is it one every reasonable person would share? Hume's hypothetical scenario would doubtless cause much puzzlement, but some people might suggest that, although no deception had taken place, Elizabeth had not really died but had entered some temporary comatose condition that everyone concerned had mistaken for death, while others might robustly hold that a miracle had in fact taken place, especially if the records

---

[41] Hume, *Enquiries*, X.96, pp. 122–23.   [42] Eve, 'Spit in Your Eye', pp. 1–17.
[43] Hume, *Enquiries*, X. 99, p. 128.

showed that in the month following her death there had been a concerted campaign of prayer for her revival. In other words, one's judgement on the case might well be affected by its broader narrative context, and some people might find it more credible as a miracle (because the context suggested a reason for divine action) than as mere anomaly (a seemingly impossible event that occurred for no apparent reason whatsoever).

Hume also fails to consider cases in which one experiences a seeming miracle (or anomaly) for oneself. Is one then to regard oneself as such a knave or a fool that one should discount the testimony of one's own senses? One might, of course, question one's sanity or one's memory or one's interpretation of what one witnessed, but having questioned, might not one still conclude that one had in fact experienced a seemingly inexplicable event? What one would be weighing here would not be so much the evidence as one's beliefs (one's belief in the veracity of one's own experience against the seeming impossibility of the supposed event), and here different people might reasonably come to different conclusions. Similar considerations might apply should one be confronted with an account of an anomalous occurrence from an eyewitness one knows well and strongly believes to be sane, honest, and reliable. When trust in oneself or other sources one regards as wholly trustworthy comes into conflict with trust in one's knowledge of what is or is not possible according to 'the laws of nature', not everyone will feel obliged to come down on the side of Hume's robust scepticism. At the very least, one may be left in a real state of doubt, as Hume allows in more mundane cases of mutual destruction of conflicting evidence.

There does, of course, come a point when our knowledge of what is or is not the case necessarily outweighs any testimony that appears to contradict it. To adapt Hume's Queen Elizabeth example, suppose we were to be told by the most impeccable source imaginable that Queen Elizabeth II rose from the dead and resumed her reign on 1 November 2022, we should still not believe it since we know it to be false; we know for a fact (about as securely as we know anything) that Queen Elizabeth II remains dead and that King Charles III now reigns in her stead; that we could have been systematically deceived on such matters seems beyond belief. There thus comes a point when knowledge we believe to be incorrigible (for all practical purposes) must outweigh any evidence to the contrary.

The issue is then whether our knowledge of the laws of nature and the impossibility of there being an exception to them have the status of being such incorrigible facts, and here opinions differ. It could reasonably be argued that our understanding of nature is constantly evolving so that the laws of nature are not facts but hypotheses, and that the constancy of the laws of nature is not a fact established by experience (for how could experience ever verify it?) but rather a necessary postulate for constructing hypotheses about how the world works. The invariability of the laws of nature is something we need to assume in order to do good science; it cannot therefore be something proved by science without invoking a circular argument. It might be countered that the success of science in explaining the world we live in justifies this assumption to the point of effectively verifying it, but it may be countered in turn that this may be an illusion fostered by focussing on phenomena that are relatively susceptible to neat scientific explanations at the expense of many others which may not be.[44]

Yet even allowing that our belief in the constancy of the laws of nature (and hence the impossibility of any anomaly that might contradict them) is an assumption rather than something we can claim to know as a fact, is it an assumption we can readily dispense with when faced with assessing accounts of the seemingly impossible or would dispensing with it risk sawing off the epistemological branch on which we're sitting (since without it, we're left with no sure means of distinguishing sense from nonsense)? This question can hardly be answered in the abstract, since the answer will vary from person to person and from culture to culture. It may also vary from one purported anomaly to another. At this point all we can say in general is that many people will find anomalies difficult to swallow, that it is reasonable to be sceptical about them, and therefore that it is justified for the inherent implausibility of anomaly to weigh heavily in the balance when particular miracle claims are being assessed, but this is not as yet either the complete or the final answer, since there some more steps we need to take first.[45]

4.3 Non-Binary Outcomes

The first of these steps is to avoid the too-ready assumption that miracle accounts must always be either straightforwardly true or straightforwardly false. For example, one occasionally comes across people suggesting that the alternatives are either the gospel miracle stories are literally true or the Evangelists are lying. This misstep is compounded when all Jesus's reported healings, exorcisms, and raisings from the dead are lumped together with his stilling of a storm, walking on the Sea of Galilee, and turning water into wine as 'miracles' which are then (by the incautious) regarded as true or false as a totality.

---

[44] See, for example, the distinction between clouds and clocks in Popper, *Objective Knowledge*, pp. 206–22.
[45] For a summary of Hume's arguments, see Swinburne, *Concept of Miracle*, pp. 13–21. For sustained criticism of these arguments and the ensuing sceptical tradition, see Keener, *Miracles*, pp. 171–208 and McGrew, 'Of Miracles', pp. 152–73. For a more positive appraisal, see Levine, 'Philosophers on Miracles', pp. 291–306 and Flew, 'Neo-Humean Arguments about the Miraculous', pp. 29–57.

In fact, there is no real difficulty in supposing that Jesus gained a significant reputation as a healer and exorcist, not least because such things have been well attested elsewhere.[46] That is not to say that every healing and exorcism story in all four gospels must be taken as factually accurate in every detail as if it were a photographic record of precisely what took place, but rather that the general impression created by these stories may well be a reasonable reflection of Jesus's healing ministry.

This leaves a relatively small residue of miracle stories involving clearly problematic anomalies. It is not normally possible for a human being to still a storm by word of command (Mark 4:35-41), walk on water (Mark 6:45-52), feed large crowds with a meagre supply of loaves and fishes (Mark 6:30-44; 8:1-10), or turn water into wine (John 2:1-12). But in assessing these stories, the options are not limited to either (1) the Bible is the Word of God and hence an impeccably reliable source, so these events must have taken place exactly as described, or (2) we know for sure that such things cannot happen so these accounts must be simply false.

Other possibilities include (3) the events happened more or less as described but have a perfectly natural explanation that was misunderstood at the time (an approach that was more fashionable a couple of centuries ago than it is today), or (4) some historical event underlay at least some of these stories, but the stories have grown in the telling, through some combination of the workings of individual and collective memory and conscious theological or typological interpretation,[47] or (5) the stories weren't intended to be taken entirely literally, but to convey other kinds of truth by symbolic means (perhaps suggested by Mark 4:11 and the symbolism that appears attached to several of his miracle stories).[48]

These possibilities are not mutually exclusive, and different ones may apply to different cases, but the last of them raises one further point, and that is that we need to consider the genre (and hence composition and reception conventions) of any given miracle story or the wider narrative context in which it occurs. Again, this is not a matter of a simple binary opposition between fact and fiction, but also of the conventions surrounding avowedly factual genres such as history and biography, which may not always follow those of the post-Enlightenment West in all times and places. For example, writers of ancient biographies (or *bioi*) and histories were allowed (or at least exercised) rather more artistic license than their counterparts in the modern Western academy and were sometimes interested in different levels of truth than pedantic adherence to

---

[46] Eve, *Healer*, pp. 63–68; Eve, *Jewish Context*, pp. 368–76.   [47] Eve, 'Growth', pp. 67–76.
[48] Eve, *Healer*, pp. 104–16, 150–56.

facts (which might not, in any case, have been fully recoverable). They also had different aims (e.g., religious persuasion) than satisfying curiosity about precisely what took place. These are all questions that cannot be fully explored here, but they once more take us back to the nature of narrative.

4.4 Competing Narratives

4.4.1 Introduction

When Hume concluded that no testimony would suffice to establish the occurrence of a miracle unless the falsehood of the testimony would be more miraculous than the miracle testified to, he was surely being sarcastic. Having established to his own satisfaction that there may be any number of non-miraculous reasons why reports of miracles may be false, he clearly supposes that his condition for establishing the occurrence of a miracle could never be met. But we can restate his conclusion in a less prejudicial way in terms of competing narratives.

On this restatement, it becomes reasonable to believe in the occurrence of a miracle if the narrative of the miracle's occurrence is more plausible than any alternative narrative that may be offered to explain how the account of the miracle arose. In this formulation 'arose' should be understood to include the reception and transmission of the miracle account as well as its initial generation.

For example, other things being equal one will be justified in being more dismissive of a miracle story that no one believed at the time or ever since than one that has been widely credited, although widespread belief in the occurrence of a miracle is not, of course, any guarantee of its veracity (a case in point would be the widely-believed story of an angelic intervention to protect the British retreat from Mons in 1914).[49] The point is rather that widespread belief in any given miracle story is one of the factors for which any competing narrative needs to give a plausible account.

In weighing up the relative plausibility of competing narratives, all three elements of our definition of miracle need to come into play. To count as a miracle, the putative event will be seemingly inexplicable (either because it cannot be causally accounted for or because it is felt to involve too much of coincidence). It must also be attributed to divine action (possibly through an intermediary), and to be attributable to divine action, it must appear to be religiously significant and/or religiously appropriate, or in other words, the sort of thing God might reasonably be expected to do given the wider context

---

[49] For which, see Machen, *The Angels of Mons*.

both of the purported event and of what is known or believed about God (from the perspective of the particular monotheistic faith of the person assessing the account). We should now examine how all these factors can help us decide whether and when it might be reasonable to believe that a miracle has occurred.

4.4.2 Inexplicability

For the purposes of this argument, 'otherwise seemingly inexplicable' means either (1) a direct violation of a fundamental law of nature or (2) lacking any plausible natural causation or (3) too much of a coincidence. What counts as too much of a coincidence will be relative to the plausibility of any special divine action, and there will inevitably be a measure of subjectivity in how this is weighed. Cases where a fundamental law of nature would need to have been breached may turn out to be rare; few miracle stories involve travelling faster than the speed of light or breaching Heisenberg's uncertainty principle. Far more common will be cases where a plausible natural explanation is lacking because it appears impossible (or at least overwhelming improbable) that the alleged event could have occurred spontaneously, and it would have been beyond human ability to bring it about given the technology available at the time.

Other things being equal, the more inexplicable a purported event appears to be, the stronger the reason for supposing it to have involved a miracle will appear, but the stronger the evidence for its occurrence would need to be for it to be reasonable to believe it had actually occurred. Other things again being equal, direct violations of a fundamental law of nature may feel more inexplicable than events that otherwise lack any clear natural causal explanation, which in turn may feel more troublesome than improbable coincidences.

We may note in passing that Hume's conception of the laws of nature seems too weak to bear the weight he wishes to place on it. Given what Hume elsewhere says about causation and the problem of induction, his notion of the laws of nature seems to be little more than that of commonly observed regularities, which then give rise to the expectation that the future will resemble the past (although he may also have had Newtonian mechanics in mind). More recent notions of the fundamental laws of nature are based on developing elegant mathematical equations that match a wide range of observations (or deductions) about the deep structure of reality in a way that accounts for what we experience at the normal human scale around us; this is less like a set of empirical observations about supposedly reoccurring phenomena ('all swans are white' or 'humans can't walk on unfrozen water') than a set of interlocking answers to a complex crossword puzzle, even though there remain areas such as quantum gravity where we have yet to figure out how all the clues fit together.

Modern defenders of Hume may be quick to point out that working with such a strengthened notion of the laws of nature strengthens Hume's case, especially if it is understood epistemologically (in other words, in terms of what we can claim to know as opposed to what actually is). Our current understanding of the laws of nature (i.e., our best widely accepted current scientific theories) may well stand in need of correction, but they are the best we currently have. Given our current state of knowledge, it is thus reasonable for us to employ them when assessing the plausibility of any purported event, particularly a putative miracle. To give credence to a strongly anomalous miracle on the evidence of an ancient text risks leaving us with no coherent way to distinguish truth from falsehood. The same also applies to more recent accounts where the supposed witnesses are no longer available for questioning and the other evidence seems dubious. To a lesser, but still considerable extent, it also applies in the more common case where no fundamental law of nature demonstrably needs to have been broken but plausible causal explanation is lacking.

That said, there could well be cases (such as a seemingly inexplicable recovery) where, while a natural explanation seems lacking, this could be because of our imperfect knowledge of the mechanisms involved or because nature is more complex than we supposed. So, for example, Ernst and Marie-Louise Keller, who otherwise exhibit a robust scepticism towards the possibility of miracle, nevertheless allow that the warrants for ruling out some purported miracles are tighter than for others, so that, for example, we can believe that Jesus healed the sick.[50] They go on to list a range of phenomena 'in the realm of psychology and parapsychology' and suggest that 'We shall perhaps discover that more things are possible in this sphere than the enlightened mind generally accepts'. They point out that 'these manifestations are not, according to the scientific view, actually miracles; that is to say, they are not empirically absolutely inexplicable events which force us to believe in the intervention of a supernatural world; they remain still unexplained *earthly* phenomena'.[51] In other words, seemingly bizarre events may occur without being miraculous because nature may be odder than we suppose. The point is well made, but one should also note that the occurrence of such a rare, seemingly odd, and poorly understood phenomenon in a religiously significant context might still count as at least a coincidence miracle, and that at least some seemingly miraculous cures (e.g., ones that might count towards canonization by the Roman Catholic Church) undergo rigorous expert medical scrutiny to rule out any possibility of a natural explanation.[52]

---

[50] Keller & Keller, *Miracles in Dispute*, pp. 201–202.
[51] Keller & Keller, *Miracles in Dispute*, pp. 202–203.
[52] On this latter point, see Woodward, *Book of Miracles,* pp. 367–70.

Against the seeming implausibility of an inexplicable event must be weighed the strength of the evidence in its favour. The evidence of our own senses or of testimonies from sources we have good reason to trust, especially if such sources are multiple and independent, could potentially outweigh our natural scepticism about the seemingly inexplicable. Several factors may influence our judgement of plausibility. These may include our judgement of the reliability of the witnesses, the factors influencing the transmission of the story (e.g., whether it reached the form in which we now have it through a process of oral transmission in which both individual and collective memory are likely to have played a part in reshaping the story), the genre of the story or the larger work in which it is embedded, and the context in which the supposed miracle is alleged to have taken place. Other factors might include the effects of the purported miracle. For example, one reason many Christians may find it easier to believe in the resurrection of Jesus than that of the many saints who were said to emerge from their tombs and walk around Jerusalem thereafter (Matt. 27:53) is that the former helps to account for the birth of the primitive church while the latter has left no historical trace whatsoever. Other factors may enter into judgements of plausibility in other cases, and such other factors may include further interlocking narratives that impinge directly (as in the example of the growth of the church) or indirectly (insofar as such narratives may influence or encapsulate our understanding of the way things work) on our assessment of the miracle story in question.[53]

Judging whether a seemingly inexplicable event could in fact have happened will not always be easy. There may be some purported miracles that strike us as so implausible and/or so poorly evidenced that we need feel little hesitation in dismissing them. There may be a few where the evidence for their occurrence strikes us as so compelling that we feel obliged to accept them. Many cases will fall into neither category, and it will then be a matter of individual judgement where we must simply do the best we can to avoid the extremes of undue scepticism (such as demanding that the evidence be beyond any reasonable doubt) and wishful thinking (believing something mainly because we'd like it to be true).

So far, however, we have only looked at one half of the story, since the plausibility of any miracle depends not only on our being able to counter justified scepticism about the seemingly inexplicable but also on our assessment of the religious appropriateness of the purported event.

---

[53] For a fuller, and more technical, account of how one might weigh conflicting evidence in such cases, see Swinburne, *Concept of Miracle*, pp. 33–51.

4.4.3 Religious Significance

C.F.D. Moule asks where we should look for consistency in relation to what might be possible and suggests that for theists the answer lies not 'in an impersonal system of causation' but rather 'in the power of God' (and that for the Christian, 'the character of God is best seen in the person of Jesus').[54] The point is well made, but note how Moule has to introduce a specifically Christian view in order for his answer to have any specific content.

Operating from a bare monotheistic context is not in itself sufficient to render an otherwise inexplicable event plausible absent the specifics of one's monotheistic beliefs. That God could in principle do anything God chooses does not tell us what God might choose to do. It might, for example, be plausibly argued that God's care for creation entails God's choosing to maintain its working in a consistent and predictable manner according to God's own design for some combination of artistry, respect for the autonomy of creation, and to allow sentient creatures to act in a morally responsible fashion, which necessitates their occupying a stable environment. Simply to be told that God is all-powerful, all-knowing, and all-loving does not tell us whether God considers it more loving to uphold a consistently stable order or to act on occasion to produce a seemingly inexplicable effect. This can only be assessed from within the context of specific religious traditions, which will be narrower not only than theism in general but also than any of the individual theistic religions. For example, Roman Catholics may be rather more inclined to accept the veracity of recent healing miracles at Lourdes than Protestants of a dispensationalist persuasion who hold that true miracles occurred only in biblical and apostolic times.

From the perspective of a particular religious tradition with specific notions of the character of God, it may well be possible to assess whether a purported miracle occurs in a religiously significant and appropriate context. We illustrated this previously with our invented example of Sally's kettle. It might be appropriate for God to act to give Sally a sign if this will help her make a life-changing decision (although one may question the need for something quite so dramatic), but it would surely be quite inappropriate to imagine the Christian God simply playing a prank on Sally or indulging her taste for wine. Similarly, God might respond to a prayer for money for a good cause by arranging for the petitioner to acquire a winning lottery ticket, but the God of any of the three Abrahamic religions can hardly be conceived of doing the same to enhance the selfish pleasures of an already over-rich plutocrat. It may be that the criterion of religious significance or appropriateness can more often be securely used to rule out purported miracles than to justify belief in them.

---

[54] Moule, 'Introduction', pp. 13–17.

This criterion can also prove problematic even when it might support belief in a miracle. Suppose Smith, a normally careful and conscientious pastor, uncharacteristically leaves her passport behind when setting out for the airport, and that a minor motor accident along her route delays her drive home to retrieve it, so that she misses her flight, and that the flight subsequently crashes killing everyone on board. Suppose also that Smith, her family, her friends, and her congregation have all prayed for her to have a safe journey. All these people might well conclude that God has worked a coincidence miracle on her behalf. But what if Jones, an equally conscientious and prayed-for pastor perishes on the very same flight. Does Smith's deliverance still seem like a miracle, or does it now appear more like pure luck? It may be argued that God had good reasons for saving Smith but not Jones, but absent knowing those reasons we may feel less confident that Smith's lucky escape should be reckoned a miracle. And what about the 300 other passengers who perished on that flight? Was none of them worthy of God's deliverance? Suppose one of them was a devout diplomat on a last-ditch mission to avert a costly war. Why would God save Pastor Smith from premature death while allowing vital peace talks to collapse? Smith might robustly continue to believe that God had worked a miracle on her behalf, but might others less directly involved be wholly unjustified in suspecting a measure of self-deception or confirmation bias on her part?

Dismissing a putative miracle as pure luck is harder to do in cases where the alleged event is of the causally inexplicable kind, but this comes at the cost of making the event's occurrence less plausible in the first place. It may still be, however, that the evidence for it appears sufficiently compelling (e.g., because one has witnessed it for oneself or received first-hand testimony from an unimpeachable source) that one feels justified in accepting its occurrence, particularly if the supposed miracle occurs in a religiously appropriate manner and context.

Where the evidence is moderately strong but less than totally compelling, one may need to weigh the implausibility of the event not only against the strength of the evidence for its occurrence but the appropriateness of explaining it as a divinely caused miracle. At this point different people may weigh the various factors involved in different ways.

We may nevertheless suggest a couple of pointers that could aid the weighing process. The first of these is that the problem of evil becomes less acute if there are (possibly self-imposed) limitations on how far God can or is willing to directly intervene in the course of events. That God can in principle do anything God wishes does not mean that God can do so in a way that is fully consistent with God's purposes, as we have already suggested. It is at least conceivable that God would regard too much interference in the normal course of events as ultimately self-defeating, for example, because it might undermine the integrity of God's creation that God wishes to maintain or the freedom of God's creatures to act in a morally accountable way. That God did not intervene miraculously to avert the Holocaust, two world wars, and a whole host of other catastrophic events in human history would seem to suggest that God must be working within some such limitations, even if we cannot say precisely what they are or what would count as 'too much interference'. One might perhaps tentatively suggest that God tends to limit miraculous interventions to those cases that are relatively with the grain of creation and involve only minimal disruption to the normal course of events.

A second, related, consideration points in much the same direction. That is the otherwise seemingly arbitrary injustice of God intervening to help some people but not others, say by miraculously healing Smith in response to prayer while leaving Jones to suffer a long and painful death. To be sure, one can always appeal to the mysteries of God's design or the different spiritual effects in different cases, but this risks attempting to explain the unknown by the unknowable. This may again suggest that God is relatively parsimonious with miracles, and also perhaps that miracles should be seen more as acts of grace than responses to human desert.

Both suggested pointers are admittedly speculative, but together, they may at least suggest another criterion that might be applied, namely that for a miracle to be plausible, the scale of the miracle should not be disproportionate to its supposed divine purpose. How easy it would be to apply this criterion in anything remotely like an objective manner is another question.

It should be noted in passing that miracles may appear more frequently among some believing communities than others, particularly in faith communities that set a relatively high store by miraculous occurrences. Believers belonging to such traditions might well question the assertion that God is parsimonious with miracles. This raises a whole series of questions about the role of faith, the way potentially miraculous events are interpreted, and the psychosocial dynamics of faith communities, all of which would need to the subject of a very different study.

One final question that can be raised here is how far we can legitimately speak of divine intentionality without anthropomorphizing God. Even if this appears unavoidable if we are to talk about monotheism and miracle at all, it once again raises the question of divine intentionality in relation to miracle. Is something ultimately a miracle because God intends it to be, or simply because one or more human beings perceive it as such? Presumably most religious believers will want to claim the former, but even if it is legitimate to speak of divine intentionality (as if God resembled human agents in this respect), how can we know what God's intentions are independently of the religious tradition in which we stand and the way in which we interpret the significant events in our lives in the light of our beliefs?

4.4.4 Two Modest Proposals

A large element of subjectivity is thus inescapable when we come to weigh the competing narratives surrounding putative miracles.[55] That does not, however, mean that anything goes and that it is all simply a matter of personal taste. The subjectivity involved is not so much a matter of individual idiosyncrasies as that of the faith tradition in which one stands, one's cultural context, and the habits of thought and judgement developed over a lifetime within that context. Yet even if different people are likely to come to different conclusions over purported miracles, they can still debate the issues involved.

The first modest proposal, then, is that, even though we cannot eliminate subjectivity from our discussion of miracle, we can at least aim to reduce it by striving to be honest (by doing our best to avoid bias and special pleading) in the way we think about these things. One way to do this might be to approach any miracle account in a four-stage process, which encapsulates what has been discussed in more detail earlier. The first stage is to ask whether the account intends to describe an event that actually occurred, or whether it primarily serves some other purpose (on which see Section 2.3.4). The second, if we decide that the story does purport to describe a real event, is to recognize that any description of a real event necessarily involves an element of interpretation by the original observers and subsequent narrators, so that one should recognize that the account is not a photographic record of what took place and may require further careful interpretation before we decide what it claims. The third is then to assess the plausibility of the event as if we lived in a closed naturalistic universe by employing the criterion of the level playing field, namely, how much credence we would give to this account if it did not come from our own religious tradition, and whether we would believe in its occurrence if divine action were not a possible explanation for it. The purpose of this stage is not to determine our conclusion by prematurely excluding the seemingly inexplicable, but to arrive at our best estimate of the degree of apparent implausibility (or seeming inexplicability) of the miracle account and the cogency of the testimony in its favour. The fourth and final stage is then to consider the wider narrative context to see if the supposed miracle is something that might

---

[55] See also Tennant, *Miracle*, pp. 73–75; cf. Woodward, *Book of Miracles*, pp. 384–85, 'Miracles, in other words, demonstrate the postmodern principle that truth (especially religious truth) is always embedded in social construction.'

reasonably be attributed to God given our beliefs about God and whether the seeming appropriateness of the miracle outweighs its apparent implausibility.

The second modest proposal is simply that we should recognize that we are never all going to agree on our assessments of the miraculous, so that rather than berating one another for our different opinions, we should treat those we disagree with respect rather than dismissing them as either credulous simpletons or unbelieving sceptics. Let us by all means continue to debate, but to do so without charity can hardly be the best way to exhibit our loyalty to the religious tradition in which we claim to stand.

4.5 How Much Does It Matter?

We have spent quite some time asking how we might decide whether miracles can actually occur and whether any given miracle actually happened, because this is a question many people are likely to want an answer to, but it is also worth asking how much it really matters to monotheistic belief.

For many religious believers, miracle may in practice (if not also in theory) be something effectively peripheral to their faith. Monotheistic faith is not primarily faith in miracles but faith in God, and how that is worked out in believers' faithfulness to God, their relationship with God, their values, their way of life, and their relationship to other people and the world around them. However much they may or may not appreciate the miraculous, miracles are unlikely to be the sole or main reason for coming to faith, which is more likely to be a result of upbringing, social and cultural environment, or attraction to a particular notion of the divine and the values and way of life it entails, or perhaps to a particular style of worship or set of customs. This is not simply a modern liberal western view; the same could, for example, be said of many of Jesus's Jewish contemporaries.[56] No doubt many contemporary Jews, Muslims, and Christians would agree; true religion is more about a way of life in obedience to God's commands or in response to God's love than worrying about whether certain seemingly inexplicable events actually occurred.

Moreover, as noted earlier, many miracle stories may have a point other than, or at least beyond, the question of whether they describe an event that literally occurred. They may, for example, disclose something about the nature of God, such that God is the source of true life, or that God desires the salvation of God's creatures, or that God is on the side of the poor and oppressed, or that God is ultimately in control, or that those who trust in God can achieve the seemingly impossible against the odds through, for example, a 'miracle' of social transformation such as achieving effective action against climate change against the

---

[56] Eve, *Jewish Context*, pp. 243–44.

inertia of governments and the vested interests of polluting producers. A story of disruption of the natural order may be a way of indicating that what seems to be a natural social order doesn't have to be that way.[57]

In any case, miracles may often be a poor prop for faith, which should ultimately be about trust in God and adherence to a particular religious tradition rather than reliance on seemingly spectacular events.[58] Moreover, while in many cases a (real or apparent) miracle may be psychologically persuasive to a given individual under particular circumstances, appeal to miracle cannot logically be used to compel belief, since it is always open to the unbeliever to dismiss any account of a putative miracle as simply false or exaggerated or as due to (possibly as yet unknown) natural causes, or a clever illusion, or, if all else fails, to some superhuman but still natural agency (such as a race of superpowerful aliens) on the basis that one cannot logically infer an infinite power from a finite effect. There is no such thing as a miracle the occurrence of which all reasonable people have felt compelled to accept.

That all said, one must be careful about legislating such matters for all believers from the perspective of contemporary Western academia (which is, of course, Keener's point). Concrete miracles may well be a far more pressing issue to people facing real deprivation, oppression, and sickness in the absence of good government and adequate healthcare. One can hardly complain if people who feel humanly helpless find their faith strengthened by miracles that offer them at least some hope of salvation and deliverance in the here and now. Moreover, even in the modern West (let alone the rest of the world), there are some miracles (such as, for Christianity, the Resurrection of Jesus) that are far more fundamental to faith than others (1 Cor. 15:17). To say that miracles may not be central to everyone's faith is by no means to dismiss them as unimportant.

5 Conclusion

We have suggested that a miracle is best defined as an otherwise seemingly inexplicable event that is understood to be an act of God in a religiously significant and appropriate context. This makes miracle a fundamentally narrative category insofar as there can be no miracle independently of the story in which it is embedded. We have also suggested that narrative may offer a better model for understanding how God relates to God's creation than the clockmaker

---

[57] See Crossley, 'The Nature Miracles as Pure Myth', and Zimmerman, 'Re-Counting the Impossible', pp. 86–106, 107–27 respectively, and Keller & Keller, *Miracles in Dispute*, 226–50.
[58] See, for example, John 2:23–25; 4:48; 6:26; 12:36–37; 20:29; and Woods, 'The Evidential Value of the Biblical Miracles', pp. 21–32.

model (although other forms of artistic creativity, such as drama and musical composition, could also be helpful analogies).

It is one thing to recognize when a particular story purports to narrate a miracle, and quite another to decide whether the purported miracle actually occurred. We have seen that the question 'do miracles occur?' can hardly be answered in the abstract, since there is no generally agreed definition of what constitutes a miracle, and even if we restrict ourselves to the definition offered here, there is an irreducible element of subjectivity in assessing miracle claims, not least because there is no neutral stance from which to issue an objective judgement. Hume may very well be right to argue that no system of religion can be founded (solely) on a supposed miracle, since the assessment of any supposed miracle will inevitably come from the perspective of one's faith tradition (be that a monotheistic or other religious tradition or belief in secular humanism and a closed naturalistic universe). From a monotheistic perspective, however, one can surely say that events have occurred and do occur that believers can quite reasonably regard as miracles. To say that is not to recommend naïve credulity or to deny the rightful place of a healthy scepticism towards the seemingly inexplicable, but simply to assert the reality of miracle in the only way it can be asserted, namely in the reception of miracle stories by those who interpret them as signs disclosing something of God's nature and God's care for God's creatures.

Bibliography

Basinger, David, 'What Is a Miracle', in Graham Twelftree (ed.), *The Cambridge Companion to Miracles* (Cambridge: Cambridge University Press, 2011), pp. 19–35.

Crossley, James, 'The Nature Miracles as Pure Myth', in Graham H. Twelftree (ed.), *The Nature Miracles of Jesus: Problems, Perspectives and Prospects* (Eugene, OR: Wipf and Stock, 2017), pp. 86–106.

Eve, Eric, *The Jewish Context of Jesus' Miracles* (Sheffield: Sheffield Academic Press, 2002).

Eve, Eric, 'Spit in Your Eye: The Blind Man of Bethsaida and the Blind Man of Alexandria', *New Testament Studies* 54 (2008), 1–17.

Eve, Eric, *The Healer from Nazareth: Jesus' Miracles in Historical Context* (London: SPCK, 2009).

Eve, Eric, 'The Growth of the Nature Miracle Stories' and Section 9.2 of 'Dialog: A Way Forward', in Graham H. Twelftree (ed.), *The Nature Miracles of Jesus: Problems, Perspectives and Prospects* (Eugene, OR: Wipf and Stock, 2017), pp. 66–85, 200–204.

Flew, Anthony, 'Neo-Humean Arguments about the Miraculous', in Douglas Geivett & Gary R. Habermas (eds.), *In Defense of Miracles: A Comprehensive Case for God's Action in History* (Downers Grove, IL: InterVarsity Press, 1997), pp. 29–57.

Glasswell, Mark Errol, 'The Use of Miracles in the Markan Gospel', in Charles Francis Digby Moule (ed.), *Miracles: Cambridge Studies in their Philosophy and History* (London: Mowbrays, 1965), pp. 151–62.

Heil, John Paul, *Jesus Walking on the Sea: Meaning and Gospel Functions of Matt 14:22–33, Mark 6:45–52 and John 6:15b–21* (Rome: Biblical Institute Press, 1981).

Hesse, Mary, 'Miracles and the Laws of Nature', in Charles Francis Digby Moule (ed.), *Miracles: Cambridge Studies in Their Philosophy and History* (London: Mowbrays, 1965), pp. 35–42.

Hume, David, *Enquiries Concerning Human Understanding and Concerning the Principles of Morals*, 3rd ed. (Oxford: Clarendon Press, 1975 [1777]).

Keener, Craig S. *Miracles: The Credibility of the New Testament Accounts*, 2 Vols. (Grand Rapids, MI: Baker Academic, 2011).

Keller, Ernst & Marie-Luise Keller, *Miracles in Dispute: A Continuing Debate* (London: SCM, 1969).

Koperski, Jeffrey, *Divine Action, Determinism, and the Laws of Nature* (London: Routledge, 2020).

Larmer, Robert A., 'The Meanings of Miracle', in Graham Twelftree (ed.), *The Cambridge Companion to Miracles* (Cambridge: Cambridge University Press, 2011), pp. 36–53.

Levine, Michael P., 'Philosophers on Miracles', in Graham Twelftree (ed.), *The Cambridge Companion to Miracles* (Cambridge: Cambridge University Press, 2011), pp. 291–306.

Levine, Michael P. 'Miracles and the Laws of Nature', in Graham Twelftree (ed.), *The Nature Miracles of Jesus: Problems, Perspectives and Prospects* (Eugene, OR: Wipf and Stock, 2017), pp. 128–51.

McGrew, Timothy, 'Of Miracles', in Graham Twelftree (ed.), *The Nature Miracles of Jesus: Problems, Perspectives and Prospects* (Eugene, OR: Wipf and Stock, 2017), pp. 152–73.

Machen, Arthur, *The Angels of Mons: The Bowmen and Other Legends of the War*, 2nd ed. (London: Simpkin, Marshall, Hamilton, Kent, 1915).

MacRae, George, 'Miracle in the *Antiquities* of Josephus', in Charles Francis Digby Moule, (ed.), *Miracles: Cambridge Studies in Their Philosophy and History* (London: Mowbrays, 1965), pp. 129–47.

Moberly, R. Walter L., 'Miracles in the Hebrew Bible', in Graham H. Twelftree (ed.), *The Cambridge Companion to Miracles* (Cambridge: Cambridge University Press, 2011), pp. 57–74.

Moule, Charles Francis Digby (ed.), *Miracles: Cambridge Studies in Their Philosophy and History* (London: Mowbrays, 1965).

Moule, Charles Francis Digby, 'Introduction', in Charles Francis Digby Moule (ed.), *Miracles: Cambridge Studies in their Philosophy and History* (London: Mowbray, 1965), pp. 1–17.

Novakovic, Lidija, 'Miracles in Second Temple and Early Rabbinic Judaism', in Graham Twelftree, (ed.), *The Cambridge Companion to Miracles* (Cambridge: Cambridge University Press, 2011), pp. 95–112.

Popper, Karl R., *Objective Knowledge: An Evolutionary Approach*, revised ed. (Oxford: Clarendon, 1979).

Ross, John P., 'Some Notes on Miracle in the Old Testament', in Charles Francis Digby Moule (ed.), *Miracles: Cambridge Studies in Their Philosophy and History* (London: Mowbrays, 1965), pp. 45–60.

Sayers, Dorothy L., *The Mind of the Maker*, 2nd ed. (London: Methuen, 1941).

Seeskin, Kenneth, 'Miracles in Jewish Philosophy', in Graham Twelftree (ed.), *The Cambridge Companion to Miracles* (Cambridge: Cambridge University Press, 2011), pp. 254–70.

Stroup, George W., *The Promise of Narrative Theology* (London: SCM, 1984).

Swinburne, Richard, *The Concept of Miracle* (London: Macmillan, 1970).

Tennant, Frederick Robert, *Miracle and Its Philosophical Presuppositions: Three Lectures Delivered at the University of London, 1924* (Cambridge: Cambridge University Press, 1925).

Thomas, David, 'Miracles in Islam', in Graham H. Twelftree (ed.), *The Cambridge Companion to Miracles* (Cambridge: Cambridge University Press, 2011), pp. 199–215.

Twelftree, Graham H., *Jesus the Miracle Worker* (Downers Grove, IL: IVP, 1999).

Twelftree, Graham H. (ed.), *The Cambridge Companion to Miracles* (Cambridge: Cambridge University Press, 2011).

Twelftree, Graham (ed.), *The Nature Miracles of Jesus: Problems, Perspectives and Prospects* (Eugene, OR: Wipf and Stock, 2017).

Wells, Herbert George, *Tales of the Unexpected* (London: Collins, 1954).

Woods, George Frederick, 'The Evidential Value of the Biblical Miracles', in Charles Francis Digby Moule (ed.), *Miracles: Cambridge Studies in Their Philosophy and History* (London: Mowbrays, 1965), pp. 21–32.

Woodward, Kenneth L., *The Book of Miracles*: *The Meaning of the Miracle Stories in Christianity, Judaism, Buddhism, Hinduism and Islam* (New York: Touchstone, 2001).

Zimmerman, Ruben, Section 9.4 of 'Dialog – A Way Forward', in Graham H. Twelftree (ed.), *The Nature Miracles of Jesus: Problems, Perspectives and Prospects* (Eugene, OR: Wipf and Stock, 2017), pp. 207–12.

Zimmerman, Ruben, 'Re-Counting the Impossible: A Literary-Hermeneutical Approach to the Nature Miracles', in Graham H. Twelftree (ed.) *The Nature Miracles of Jesus: Problems, Perspectives and Prospects* (Eugene, OR: Wipf and Stock, 2017), pp. 107–27.

Cambridge Elements

Religion and Monotheism

Paul K. Moser
Loyola University Chicago

Paul K. Moser is Professor of Philosophy at Loyola University Chicago. He is the author of *God in Moral Experience; Paul's Gospel of Divine Self-Sacrifice; The Divine Goodness of Jesus; Divine Guidance; Understanding Religious Experience; The God Relationship; The Elusive God* (winner of national book award from the Jesuit Honor Society); *The Evidence for God; The Severity of God; Knowledge and Evidence* (all Cambridge University Press); and *Philosophy after Objectivity* (Oxford University Press); coauthor of *Theory of Knowledge* (Oxford University Press); editor of *Jesus and Philosophy* (Cambridge University Press) and *The Oxford Handbook of Epistemology* (Oxford University Press); and coeditor of *The Wisdom of the Christian Faith* (Cambridge University Press). He is the coeditor with Chad Meister of the book series *Cambridge Studies in Religion, Philosophy, and Society*.

Chad Meister
Affiliate Scholar, Ansari Institute for Global Engagement with Religion, University of Notre Dame

Chad Meister is Affiliate Scholar at the Ansari Institute for Global Engagement with Religion at the University of Notre Dame. His authored and co-authored books include *Evil: A Guide for the Perplexed* (Bloomsbury Academic, 2nd edition); *Introducing Philosophy of Religion* (Routledge); *Introducing Christian Thought* (Routledge, 2nd edition); and *Contemporary Philosophical Theology* (Routledge). He has edited or co-edited the following: *The Oxford Handbook of Religious Diversity* (Oxford University Press); *Debating Christian Theism* (Oxford University Press); with Paul Moser, *The Cambridge Companion to the Problem of Evil* (Cambridge University Press); and with Charles Taliaferro, *The History of Evil* (Routledge, in six volumes). He is the co-editor with Paul Moser of the book series *Cambridge Studies in Religion, Philosophy, and Society.*

About the Series

This Cambridge Element series publishes original concise volumes on monotheism and its significance. Monotheism has occupied inquirers since the time of the Biblical patriarch, and it continues to attract interdisciplinary academic work today. Engaging, current, and concise, the Elements benefit teachers, researched, and advanced students in religious studies, Biblical studies, theology, philosophy of religion, and related fields.

Cambridge Elements

Religion and Monotheism

Elements in the Series

Monotheism and Divine Aggression
Collin Cornell

Jewish Monotheism and Slavery
Catherine Hezser

Open Theism
Alan R. Rhoda

African Philosophy of Religion and Western Monotheism
Kirk Lougheed, Motsamai Molefe and Thaddeus Metz

Monotheism and Pluralism
Rachel S. Mikva

The Abrahamic Vernacular
Rebecca Scharbach Wollenberg

Monotheism and Fundamentalism: Prevalence, Potential, and Resilience
Rik Peels

Emotions and Monotheism
John Corrigan

Monotheism and Peacebuilding
John D Brewer

Monotheism and Wisdom in the Hebrew Bible: An Uneasy Pair?
James L. Crenshaw

Monotheism and Relativism
Bernd Irlenborn

Monotheism and Miracle
Eric Eve

A full series listing is available at: www.cambridge.org/er&m

www.ingramcontent.com/pod-product-compliance
Ingram Content Group UK Ltd.
Pitfield, Milton Keynes, MK11 3LW, UK
UKHW020005050225
454695UK00012B/69